COOK
ORGANIC

COOK
ORGANIC

Gilli Davies

metro

First published in Great Britain in 1998
by Metro Books (an imprint of Metro Publishing Limited), 19 Gerrard Street,
London W1V 7LA

British Library Cataloguing in Publication Data. A CIP record of this book is
available on request from the British Library.

ISBN 1 900512 36 X

10 9 8 7 6 5 4 3 2 1

Typeset by SX Composing DTP, Rayleigh, Essex
Printed in Great Britain by CPD Group, Wales

Contents

Foreword

I was delighted to have been asked to write the foreword for this excellent new book by Gilli Davies. Cooking with locally grown ingredients is one of life's greatest pleasures as they are superior in both flavour and quality to those grown intensively using chemical fertilizers and pesticides. I can vouch for this from personal experience on my farm in West Wales, which has been managed organically for more than twenty years.

As someone interested in organic food, you are in extremely good company. A recent MORI poll conducted by the Soil Association revealed that a staggering 62 per cent of the public would now prefer to buy organic food if the problems of price and availability could be overcome. Yet, amazingly, despite the ever-growing demand, we still lie near the bottom of the European league for organic farming with currently less than 0.5 per cent of our producers using organic methods.

The Soil Association has been campaigning for fifty years to promote sustainable organic farming which avoids the use of chemical fertilizers and pesticides, while protecting the environment and safeguarding animal welfare. The good news for the readers of this book is that reasonably priced organic food should become easier to find in the shops as at last our voice is being heard and the Government is beginning to take organic farming more seriously.

If you would like to add your voice to ours in our campaign for organic farming, join the Soil Association (there is a membership form at the end of this book). By doing so, you will be safeguarding your own health and helping to protect the planet for future generations.

I hope that you will make good use of this book and that it will become a central part of your kitchen reference library.

Patrick Holden
Director, Soil Association
January 1998

Introduction

Do we really need a book about how to cook organic food? Surely we can just use organic ingredients in our existing recipes?

Not so, for anyone who already buys organic food will know that there is a depth of flavour, improved texture and quality to these ingredients that simply do not exist in much of the mass-produced food of today. The intense flavour of organic ingredients requires the simplest of cooking to ensure that no goodness is lost. The recipes in this book will produce the best flavours available in food today through quick and easy preparation. From the cook's point of view, it is satisfying to know that, through the use of organic ingredients, you are doing the best to protect your health and support growers who use natural methods of production. You may notice that the recipes here have fewer ingredients than usual and this is because organic ingredients just do not need the addition of extra flavours. Do you ever consider why we struggle to add extra flavour to bland chicken breasts, why we toss almost everything into a curry sauce and why even chips are now covered in extra flavourings? Is it because modern, intensively produced foods simply do not taste as good as they used to when food was grown more naturally?

Are you worried about the increasing scares over the food we eat? What will follow BSE, how did E-coli arrive in Britain and what are genetically modified organisms? As a consumer do you want to know where your food comes from, how it has been produced and processed and what additives it contains? Should our food supplies be so reliant on intensive farming methods?

I believe for our health and the sake of food safety it is a wise decision to choose organic ingredients wherever possible – and they taste better, too! By organic ingredients I do not mean muddy carrots and insect-nibbled cabbages, but a wide range of fruits and vegetables, meat, fish, game and poultry, dairy products, eggs, tea, coffee, baby foods, cereals, pasta, olives and pickles, flour and bread, storecupboard ingredients and a host of other items ranging from exquisite Japanese Tamari to intensely flavoured chocolate.

An organic ingredient is one that has been produced:

- without the use of artificial pesticides and fertilizers;

- through a system of crop rotation – the natural method of conserving and enhancing soil fertility – rather than intensive farming;

- with care for the natural features of the landscape and preservation of wildlife habitats;

- with environmental concerns uppermost in the mind and pollution being kept to a minimum;

- with care for animal welfare and an avoidance of the routine use of antibiotics and hormone stimulants.

For the growing number of consumers who now buy organic ingredients, the benefits are easily recognized in terms of the improved flavour, the long-term effect on family health and our social conscience about animal welfare, the environment and sustainability of farming methods.

As to the cost of buying organic ingredients – yes, they are more expensive because they cost more to grow and small organic farms cannot benefit from the economics of scale enjoyed by the bigger operations. Labour costs are higher, some crop yields are lower due to the biological system where pests and diseases are controlled naturally, without chemicals. With crop rotation, the soil in each field is given time to regenerate its nutrients through crops like clover, rather than continuous corn which requires fertilizer to bump-start the soil. Non-organic foods may cost less at the supermarket checkout but what is the long-term cost to our health? Buying organically grown food supports growers who use environmentally safe production methods. And, unlike most things that are good for us, eating organic food is a tremendous pleasure.

Today, organic food is easy to find. Most of the main supermarkets carry a range of organic products. In addition, look out for dedicated suppliers, whether organic or health food shops, larger direct delivery schemes and your local box scheme, where the freshness of each ingredient is guaranteed. The list of suppliers at the end of this book will show you where to start looking.

When buying organic food, donít forget to look out for the Soil Association symbol, your guarantee of organic quality. The Soil Association has been at the centre of the campaign for safe, healthy food, an unpolluted countryside and a sustainable organic farming policy in Britain since it was formed fifty years ago. By joining the Association, you will be supporting campaigns for an increase in support for organic farming and for 'local food link distribution schemes' and to outlaw such dangerous practices as the introduction of genetic engineering, the irresponsible use of antibiotics and the use of organo-phosphate pesticides in intensive farming systems. Soil Association members also receive a quarterly award-winning magazine, *Living Earth*, and have access to over forty-five active local groups around the country.

Of course, the way to guarantee optimum freshness in food is to produce your own. There is nothing so satisfying as growing your own fruit and vegetables – the thrill of picking your first fragrant tomato straight off the vine – and even if all the space you have is a patio or balcony, you can still grow a tasty and attractive crop in pots. Or perhaps you are already a keen gardener; by learning to garden organically you can produce safe, healthy food with a minimum of damage to the environment. As with organic farming, you can help with the sustainability of the soil, and reduce pollution of the environment by recycling garden, household and other wastes, rather than dumping or burning them. Imagine the satisfaction of being able to combat pests without synthetic pesticides, and encouraging wildlife. Perhaps most important though is that buzz you get from the delicious crisp flavour of eating something you have grown, and that was still in the soil just minutes before you prepared it.

To find out more about organic gardening, join the Henry Doubleday Research Association (at Ryton Organic Gardens, Coventry CV8 3LG; Tel: 01203 303517/Fax: 01203 639229/Email: enquiry@hdra.org.uk). This is Europe's largest organic gardening association. Founded in 1958 by Lawrence D. Hills and named after the nineteenth-century Quaker small-holder who first introduced and promoted Russian comfrey in England, it is now under the direction of Alan and Jackie Gear. The gardens, along with a shop and restaurant, attract 80,000 visitors annually. Here you will find advice on everything from how to deal with slugs to how to create an organic lawn. They also produce *The Fruit and Vegetable Finder* which lists all available vegetable varieties in the UK and their suppliers.

Don't be deterred if you cannot get hold of every organic ingredient you would like to. Have a go anyway. Even if only half the ingredients you use are organically produced, you are making a start. And the more consumers buy organic foods, the more will become available in the shops.

If we are what we eat, then let's make sure that we feed ourselves with food that is good for us. Think carefully about the food you buy, and enjoy the preparation. Remember that the best ingredients usually benefit from simple cooking. Involve friends and family with testing the flavour of new ingredients, and enjoy being creative. Even in a packed schedule, there is always time for a quick snack, so make sure it's made from ingredients you believe in.

If you had the opportunity to speak to organic farmers, it would be hard to miss the passion that dominates their work and lifestyle. Let's bring some of that passion into our kitchens. For flavour, health and a sustainable environment – cook organic!

Author's Note: All recipes in this book serve 4 unless otherwise stated.

Organic Ingredients

The range of organic ingredients that are available is constantly increasing, so that the possibility for us to be able to cook and eat only organic foods is now a reality. You may, perhaps, choose to add just a few organic ingredients to your diet rather than adapt your whole lifestyle to the organic ethos but, either way, shopping for organic ingredients gets easier and easier.

Supermarkets are selling an ever increasing range (Sainsbury now boasts over fifty varieties of organic foods) particularly fresh fruit and vegetables, with some meat and dairy products like cheese and yogurt, bread, eggs, teabags, even babyfoods. There is a choice of four organic babyfood producers, from the well-known Baby Organix to Eco Baby, Hipp Organic and Babynat.

One of the most satisfying ways of buying organic vegetables is through a box scheme and I am always delighted to look through my weekly box of assorted seasonal fresh vegetables that is ready for collection every weekend locally. The items in my box range from Jerusalem artichokes, cabbage, leeks, garlic, onions, parsnips, potatoes and swedes in January, to broad and runner beans, basil, courgettes, aubergines, fennel, flowers, mixed salad leaves, peppers, spinach, sugar peas and cherry tomatoes in mid summer.

The first time I visited an organic supermarket I marvelled at the choice. If you do not have one of these dedicated shops near to you, remember that many are happy to receive orders by phone, fax or E-mail and will deliver to you wherever you are.

Alternatively, look in our list of local suppliers at the end of this book – there may be a shop or delivery service near you.

Imagine a range of fresh herbs from basil to oregano, sprouts from alfalfa to mung, and an extensive variety of exotic vegetables and fruit. Sourced locally whenever possible, there is now a selection comparable with non-organic fresh produce like apples, apricots, kiwi, mangoes, pears, pineapples and, of course, strawberries.

Organic dried fruit are well worth searching out, from apple rings to pitted dates, Hunza apricots to sweet cherries; also bottled mango, peaches and plums – even wild apricot halves.

Fresh organic bread is available, including the basic wholemeals and malted grains bread to French sticks and focaccia, sourdough, apple, raisin and cinnamon rolls, pumpernickel and sesame grissini – even Tibetan barley bread. And if you crave organic breakfast cereals these are available in abundance, ranging from Doves Farm Cornflakes to Allos Puffed Buckwheat with Honey.

Stock up your storecupboard with mustard, sauces, purées and pickles, from Zest pesto to Las Bio Ideas passata, Meridian vinegars, Whole Earth tomato ketchup and Sanchi brown rice vinegar. Look out for coarse and fine sea salt, vegetable stocks and bouillon, sun-dried tomatoes, chilli paste, mayonnaise, salad dressings, vinegars, cold-pressed oils, varying from Italian extra virgin olive oil to flaxseed oil, safflower, sunflower, sesame, hazelnut, pumpkin, walnut and even coconut fat for frying. For the hurried cook there are a range of convenience foods like organic canned sardines, soups, even pizza.

The range of fresh meat, often from Eastbrook Farm, is commendable. Graig Farm supplies many outlets too. Other suppliers of organic meat are Meat Matters, Longwood Farm and West Country Organic Foods (see the list of organic suppliers at the end of this book). You can buy organic dry-cured bacon, cuts of beef, chicken, lamb, offal, pork, even sausages. Ask your local butcher – they are increasingly aware of the demand for organically produced meat.

Fish is much harder to select. Although there is now a standard for organic wild fish (Graig Farm can supply this), there is little to prove the cleanliness of fish today. I generally avoid farmed fish and look for wild fish that has, I hope, come from unpolluted waters. The best option is to buy your fish from a knowledgeable fishmonger.

Organic cheeses and dairy products offer plenty of choice, ranging from Cheddar to cream cheese, Welsh organic and even Swedish; also crème fraîche, cream and, of course, Rachel's Dairy live yoghurts.

Buying eggs becomes increasingly complicated now that you can buy 'farm fresh' and other tempting suggestions. However, none of these guarantee the freedom of the chickens or their feed, so I stick to organic eggs if I can, or free range.

Feeling thirsty? Then you will be pleasantly surprised by the wonderful range of organic drinks available. There are organic coffees and wonderful herbal teas as well as loose Indian and China teas and teabags. Or go for fruit juices, Caledonian Brewery Golden Pale Ale and other beers, Dunkertons cider, waters and wines. There are now over 200 organic wines available, many suitable for vegetarians, in white, rosé, red and sparkling – and you won't have to go without champagne when celebrating the organic way. Choose from white Bordeaux to Italian Vino da Tavola del Veneto Chardonnay, Sonop Wine Farm Sauvignon Blanc from South Africa or DO Penedes Tempranillo Albet i Noya.

Naturally, there are many flours and baking ingredients to choose from: wholemeal, white, strong white, plus a range of less common flours like quinoa, rye, buckwheat, spelt and even carob, with Easybake yeast and polenta, too. There is also a range of cakes and waffles, biscuits, crispbreads and rice cakes.

You might well expect a good selection of pasta, rice, grains and seeds and you won't be disappointed. There are now some exciting flavours such as penne with basil, spaghetti with nettles, and even quinoa tagliatelli, spelt pasta and millet lumaconi. Brown rice, risotto rice, short grain, long grain, wild rice and even black Thai rice. Grains vary from amaranth to buckwheat, bulgar to pearl barley, popcorn to wheat grain. And if you like seeds, you will find alfalfa, linseed, pumpkin – even hemp seeds.

Some of the imported Japanese ingredients are well worth experimenting with. Look out for firm tofu, a range of miso and noodles including soba, udon and ramen. Seaweeds are good, too, and you will find arame, hijiki, kombu, nori and wakame, as well as a range of snacks such as seaweed peanuts, and hot wasabi peas. And do not forget superb sauces like Tamari soy sauce, brown rice vinegar, mirin and toasted sesame oil.

When it comes to sugar for cooking, particularly baking, I rely on Billingtons for their unrefined sugars rather than organic granulated or demerara sugar. I also use unrefined sugar cane juice, maple syrup and corn syrups, as well as fructose powder.

So, if you wished, it really would be possible to consume nothing but organic foods. Should you need encouragement, have the courage of your convictions and stock up with ingredients that you know have been produced in a way of which you approve and with which you will be happy for the sake of your enjoyment, your health and your peace of mind.

Note
Some recipes in this book use raw or undercooked eggs. While organic or free range eggs are more likely to be free of salmonella, this cannot be guaranteed, so these recipes should be avoided by the elderly, young children, pregnant women and people whose immunity has been compromised by illness.

Soups

Muddy potatoes, grubby carrots – somehow one's imagination of organic vegetables fits well into the soup section. But not so fast! Remember good soup must be made from ingredients that literally burst with flavour. There are many naturally produced ingredients to choose from. Fresh vegetables from the garden, a selection from the local organic market garden, the supermarket's best buy or gathered from the wild.

It is perhaps the extra flavours of stock, pasta, herbs, spices and garnishes that need the most attention. Stock your cupboards with the best ingredients you can find. Many – like dried miso, whole spices and dried organic pasta will keep, remember. The flavour will tell you all you need to know.

Soups are a passion with some people. They are comforting, nourishing and can be made well in advance. I have included some unusual soups here. They highlight the best organic ingredients available throughout the seasons and provide a range of soup throughout the year. If you cannot find some of the ingredients locally, then be brave – adjust the soup to the ingredients that are available. If there is one golden rule to follow when making soup, it is: follow no rules and always experiment!

Parsnip and Caraway Soup

This is a delicious soup to serve when the nights are drawing in. Sweet spicy parsnips blend well with the light aniseed flavour of caraway and, for those of us who are addicted to the mellow sweetness of parsnips, the flavour of organically grown ones will be a revelation. This soup can be made well ahead of time and improves with reheating. Serve with chunks of warm bread.

25g (1oz) butter
450g (1lb) parsnips, peeled and
  chopped
2 medium leeks, chopped and
  washed
2.5-5ml (½-1 teaspoon) caraway
  seeds, freshly ground in a spice mill

600ml (1 pint) vegetable stock
600ml (1 pint) milk
sea salt and freshly ground black
  pepper
20ml (4 teaspoons) natural yogurt, to
  serve

- Melt the butter in a large pan and cook the parsnips and leeks gently for 10 minutes. Stir in the ground caraway seeds and add the liquids and seasoning. Simmer for 20 minutes.

- Leave the soup to cool slightly before blending to a purée in a food processor or liquidizer. Reheat, then taste to check that there is enough seasoning.

- Serve in warm bowls, with 5ml (1 teaspoon) yogurt swirled on top of each serving.

Iced Ripe Tomato and Garlic Soup

This is a soup with lots of texture and flavour; perfect all summer long, but particularly good for those late balmy days when home-grown tomatoes are ripe and bursting with flavour. Although it cannot be served as a warm soup, chilled soups are quite acceptable to most of us from Easter through to the autumn.

2 cloves garlic
sea salt and freshly ground black
  pepper
75g (3oz) fresh bread, crusts
  removed
red or white wine vinegar, to taste
1kg (2¼lb) ripe tomatoes, halved
iced water
½ large cucumber, roughly chopped
1 onion, quartered

½ green pepper, deseeded
150ml (¼ pint) sunflower or safflower
  oil

For the garnish
½ cucumber, diced
½ green pepper, deseeded and diced
croûtons (toasted bread cubes)
ice cubes

- Crush the garlic with a good pinch of salt. Soak the bread in 30ml (2 tablespoons) vinegar.

- In a food processor, blend the tomatoes with 30ml (2 tablespoons) iced water. Rub the blended tomatoes through a sieve to make a purée.

- In the processor, chop the soaked bread, cucumber, onion and green pepper with the oil. Add the chilled tomato purée, season to taste with black pepper and add more iced water to give the soup the right consistency. Sharpen with more vinegar if necessary.

- Serve in chilled bowls, with the garnish ingredients floating on top of the soup or handed separately in small bowls.

Classic Welsh Country Soup

In the past, a pot of this soup would have been made from bacon that had been hanging on a hook in the kitchen to cure during the cold winter months. Today, a good smoked bacon joint has all the flavour you need. With root vegetables and herbs from the garden, what could be more natural? There's nothing quite like it on a cold winter's day.

1kg (2¼lb) piece of bacon or ham (shoulder or corner)	2 turnips
	25g (1oz) butter
1 onion, halved	1 large leek, white and green parts diced separately
4 carrots	
3 parsnips	15ml (1 tablespoon) chopped fresh winter savory or sage
1 bay leaf	
1 bunch of fresh parsley, leaves chopped and stalks reserved	sea salt and freshly ground black pepper

- Soak the bacon or ham in cold water overnight to remove some of the salt.

- Drain well and put the whole piece in a large pan with enough cold water to cover. Add the onion halves, 1 whole carrot and 1 whole parsnip, the bay leaf and parsley stalks. Simmer gently for 1 hour.

- Leave to cool, then skim the fat from the surface.

- Remove the bacon from the stock, strain the stock and reserve. Slice some of the bacon for a separate meal and cut the remainder into chunks for the soup.

- Peel and cube the remaining carrots and parsnips and the turnips. Gently fry them in the butter with the white parts of the leeks. Pour in the reserved stock and add the chunks of bacon and the chopped parsley, savory and green leek. Simmer for 20 minutes.

- Season well and serve the soup with chunks of fresh bread. Alternatively, leave overnight for the flavours to develop.

Salmon Chowder with Prawns

This is a soup with chunks of flavour and a crunchy texture – more of a meal than a first course. Wild salmon is the best choice, of course, and if you have reservations about using farmed salmon, then use naturally smoked haddock or cod. Do take care not to overcook the fish.

30-45ml (2-3 tablespoons) sunflower or safflower oil	1.2 litres (2 pints) vegetable or fish stock
1 large onion, finely chopped	225g (8oz) wild salmon, skinned, boned and cut into 1.25cm (½in) chunks
2 green peppers, deseeded and finely chopped	
2 leeks or 1 bunch of spring onions, finely chopped	225g (8oz) uncooked prawns, peeled
4 potatoes, peeled and diced	100g (4oz) cream cheese
	sea salt and freshly ground black pepper

- Heat the oil in a large pan and add the onion, peppers and leeks. Cook gently for 10 minutes so that the vegetables soften but do not brown. Add the potatoes, stock and seasoning and simmer until the potatoes are soft.

- Add the salmon and cook for 5 minutes, then add the prawns and cook for a few minutes until they turn pink. At the last minute, add the cream cheese a little at a time and blend it in. Taste and add seasoning.

- Serve at once, with chunks of fresh bread.

Spinach and Nutmeg Soup

The flavour of fresh organic spinach is superb and this soup, although simple, benefits from the best ingredients. I am always surprised just how quickly spinach wilts away, and although 2lb will seem a lot to begin with, it will soon disappear into the pan. The nutmeg adds an aromatic edge, and I love it!

25g (1oz) butter
2 medium onions, peeled and
  chopped
1 large potato, peeled and diced
900g (2lb) spinach, well washed, with
  coarse stalks removed
300ml (½ pint) chicken or vegetable
  stock
600ml (1 pint) milk

2.5ml (½ teaspoon) freshly grated
  nutmeg
sea salt and freshly ground black
  pepper

For the garnish
crème fraîche or natural yogurt
a little freshly grated nutmeg

- Melt the butter in a large pan and cook the onions and potato gently for 5 minutes until they begin to soften. Add the spinach and stir until it absorbs some of the butter and begins to wilt. Pour in the stock and milk and add the nutmeg and seasoning. Simmer gently for 20 minutes.

- Leave to cool slightly before blending to a purée in a food processor or liquidizer. Reheat, then taste to check that there is enough seasoning.

- Serve in warm bowls, with a swirl of crème fraîche or yogurt and a sprinkling of nutmeg on top.

7

Watercress Soup with Goat's Cheese Crostini

The freshness of watercress together with its bright green colour always makes a good soup. Here, the goat's cheese croûtes add a touch of salt and creaminess which adds another dimension and makes more of a meal. Goat's cheese is now widely available from supermarkets and delicatessens.

40g (1½ oz) butter
1 small onion, diced
1 large or 2 medium potatoes, peeled and cut into chunks
450g (1lb) watercress
1.2 litres (2 pints) vegetable stock

sea salt and freshly ground black pepper

For the crostini
4 slices of French bread
50g (2oz) fresh goat's cheese

- Melt the butter in a large pan and cook the onion gently until soft. Add the potato chunks, stir well until covered in butter, then add the watercress and stock. Bring to the boil and simmer gently for 20 minutes.

- Leave to cool slightly before blending to a purée in a food processor or liquidizer.

- Make the crostini: toast the French bread on one side, turn the slices over and spread the soft sides with the goat's cheese. Put under a pre-heated hot grill until the cheese is brown and crisp.

- Reheat the soup, then season to taste. Pour into warm bowls and float a crostini on top of each. Serve immediately.

Mushroom Soup with Miso and Buckwheat Noodles

This is a delicate soup in the Japanese style, based on the superb flavour of miso, a rich savoury paste made from fermented soya beans. It is very nutritious, full of living enzymes – which are good for us – and should be kept in the refrigerator. Alternatively, dried miso is readily available as a powder from most health food shops.

1.2 litres (2 pints) well-flavoured vegetable stock
1 carrot, peeled and diced
1 sweet potato or ordinary potato, peeled and diced
225g (8oz) mushrooms, finely chopped

50g (2oz) fresh or dried buckwheat noodles
sea salt
30ml (2 tablespoons) miso
finely chopped spring onion, to garnish

- Heat the stock in a pan and add the carrot and potato. Simmer for 5 minutes, then add the mushrooms and simmer for 3-4 minutes until all the vegetables are tender.

- Boil the noodles in plenty of salted water according to packet instructions until they are *al dente*. Drain the noodles, then run cold water through them to wash out the starch.

- Blend some of the hot soup stock with the miso in a small bowl, then return the mixture to the hot soup. Do not let the soup boil or the nutrients in the miso will be lost.

- Divide the noodles between 4 warm bowls and ladle the soup on top. Scatter the finely chopped spring onion over for garnish.

Avgolemono

This delicious Greek soup is made all over the Eastern Mediterranean. In Cyprus, where I first tasted it, it is traditionally served on Easter morning to break the Lenten fast. Well-flavoured stock is essential, so it is a good soup to make after you have made stock from a chicken carcass.

1.5 litres (2½ pints) well-flavoured chicken stock	juice of 1 large or 2 small lemons
50g (2oz) round-grain or long-grain rice	sea salt and freshly ground black pepper
2 eggs	30ml (2 tablespoons) finely chopped parsley or chives, to garnish

- Bring the stock to the boil in a large pan. Add the rice and simmer for 10-12 minutes until cooked. Take the pan off the heat and allow the soup to cool a little.

- Beat the eggs and lemon juice together in a bowl. Add a spoonful of the warm soup, stir well, then blend the egg mixture back into the soup, stirring all the time. Reheat the soup carefully, taking care not to let it boil or it will curdle. Taste for seasoning, and don't be afraid to add salt – this will improve the lemon flavour rather than drown it.

- Serve immediately, sprinkled with chopped parsley or chives.

Tomato and Marjoram Soup

This is the perfect recipe for high summer when tomatoes are in glut and their flavour is at its best. There is a remarkable amount of flavour in the stalks, so leave them on when making this soup. Marjoram is available all year round but its flavour is particularly keen in the summer.

2kg (4½lb) ripe tomatoes	2.5ml (½ teaspoon) sugar
45ml (3 tablespoons) olive oil	a good handful of fresh marjoram
1 medium onion or 2 shallots,	(leaves and stalks)
chopped	600ml (1 pint) vegetable stock
sea salt and freshly ground black	
pepper	

- Chop the tomatoes roughly, stalks (calyxes) and all. Keep all the juice.
- Heat the oil in a large pan and cook the onion very gently until soft. Add the tomatoes and juice, salt, pepper, sugar and most of the marjoram (keep some of the leaves for garnish). Put a lid on the pan and cook very gently over low heat for 20 minutes.
- Leave to cool slightly before blending to a purée in a food processor or liquidizer, then press the purée through a sieve into a clean pan (using a rounded ladle for this will make it easier).
- Reheat, adding enough stock to make a good consistency. Taste to check that there is enough seasoning.
- Serve hot, garnished with the reserved marjoram.

Red Hot Beetroot Soup

During the early summer when beetroot are at their best, they make a delicious, brightly coloured soup. I like to grate the vegetables so they retain a good texture in the light stock, but this can be rather messy if you grate them all by hand. A grater blade on a food processor makes light work of the job.

450g (1lb) firm raw beetroot	1.2 litres (2 pints) vegetable stock
1 medium potato	sea salt and freshly ground black
2 carrots	pepper
1 small onion or shallot	a few drops of Tabasco sauce

- Peel and grate the beetroot, potato, carrots and onion.

- Put all the vegetables in a large pan, add the stock and seasoning and bring to the boil. Simmer gently for 20 minutes until the beetroot and carrots are soft.

- Taste for seasoning and add a few drops of Tabasco to add some fiery heat.

- Serve the soup in white bowls for preference – so the splendid colour of the beetroot shines out.

Fennel and Lemongrass Soup

A fragrant mixture of the aniseed vegetable fennel with a tang of oriental lemongrass. Use bulb fennel rather than its feathery offshoot because the flavour is more subtle and the leaves make a great garnish or salad ingredient. This soup takes only 20 minutes to prepare and is a great way to get the very best flavours out of the ingredients.

3 bulbs of fennel	2 fresh lemongrass stems
1 medium potato	sea salt and freshly ground black
2 parsnips	pepper
1 shallot or small onion, chopped	juice of ½ lemon (optional)
1.2 litres (2 pints) good vegetable	30ml (2 tablespoons) single cream, to
stock	serve

- Discard any rough outer leaves from the fennel and keep any feathery offshoots to one side to use as a garnish. Slice the fennel bulb. Peel the potato and parsnips if the skins are very rough, otherwise simply wash them well. Chop the vegetables into large chunks.

- Put all the vegetables in a large pan with the stock, lemongrass and seasoning. Bring to the boil and simmer gently for 20 minutes.

- Leave the soup to cool slightly before blending to a purée in a food processor or liquidizer. Reheat, then taste to check that there is enough seasoning, adding the lemon juice to sharpen the flavour if necessary.

- Serve in warm bowls, with a swirl of cream on top.

Prawn Gumbo

The name gumbo sounds fun, and this soup is ideal to serve for a crowd because it is much more than a soup. Gumbo is a Cajun dish, hot and spicy, with lots of ingredients to make a very satisfying meal. Serve in bowls over steamed white rice, with crusty bread to soak up the broth.

45ml (3 tablespoons) olive oil
1 onion, sliced
2 cloves garlic, crushed
1 green pepper, deseeded and sliced
15ml (1 tablespoon) plain flour
450g (1lb) ripe tomatoes, peeled and quartered, or 425g (15oz) can tomatoes
1 red pepper, deseeded and sliced
2 celery sticks, diced
1 fresh green chilli, deseeded and sliced
½ lemon, sliced
1 bay leaf

5ml (1 teaspoon) chopped fresh marjoram
5ml (1 teaspoon) paprika
2.5ml (½ teaspoon) cumin seeds, freshly ground in a spice mill
2.5ml (½ teaspoon) coriander seeds, freshly ground in a spice mill
sea salt and freshly ground black pepper
Tabasco sauce, to taste
600ml (1 pint) water
450g (1lb) cooked prawns, peeled
4 cooked jumbo prawns in their shells, to garnish
hot steamed rice, to serve

- Heat the olive oil in a large pan and fry the onion, garlic and green pepper gently until soft. Stir in the flour and cook, stirring all the time, until it turns a light brown. Add the remaining ingredients, except the prawns. Bring to the boil, then simmer very gently for 45 minutes.

- Add the peeled prawns and jumbo prawns and heat through. Taste to check that there is enough seasoning, adding more Tabasco if necessary to make the gumbo spicy.

- Serve over hot steamed rice in warm bowls, with a jumbo prawn on top of each serving.

Wakame and Miso Soup

A delicately flavoured Japanese soup, quickly prepared once you have the ingredients. It makes a great start to an oriental meal but would go well with any menu. Good organic or health food shops should have wakame seaweed and red miso but, if not, seek out a Japanese or Chinese supermarket.

1.2 litres (2 pints) well-flavoured vegetable stock 15g (½oz) dried wakame seaweed 30ml (2 tablespoons) red miso	**For the garnish** 1 small leek, finely sliced and washed 1 sheet of nori seaweed

- Heat the stock in a pan and add the wakame, breaking it into small pieces. Simmer very gently for 10 minutes.

- Put the miso in a bowl and blend in a little of the warm soup, whisking hard to make a smooth paste. Return this mixture to the pan.

- Steam the leek very quickly, either in a sieve over the soup or in a microwave oven. Rinse the cooked leek under the cold tap to retain the bright green colour.

- Toast the sheet of nori directly over a flame, then crumble it.

- Serve the soup in warm bowls, with the leek and nori added as a garnish.

Carrot and Coriander Soup

The flavours of carrot and spices are a classic and popular combination. However, this soup becomes something very special when you have the added flavour of organic carrots. When I opened my first restaurant over twenty years ago, carrot soup was the first item on the menu, and now it is still the most popular soup I make for the family.

25g (1oz) butter
1kg (2¼lb) carrots, peeled and cut into chunks
1.2 litres (2 pints) vegetable stock
5ml (1 teaspoon) grated fresh root ginger

5ml (1 teaspoon) coriander seeds, roughly crushed
sea salt and freshly ground black pepper
fresh coriander leaves, to garnish

- Melt the butter in a large pan and cook the carrots gently for 5 minutes so they absorb the flavour of the butter. Add the stock, ginger, coriander seeds and seasoning and bring to the boil. Cover the pan and simmer gently for 20 minutes.

- Leave the soup to cool slightly before blending to a purée in a food processor or liquidizer. Reheat, then taste to check that there is enough seasoning, adding more salt if necessary to bring out the flavour of the carrots.

- Serve in warm bowls, with fresh coriander leaves scattered over as a garnish.

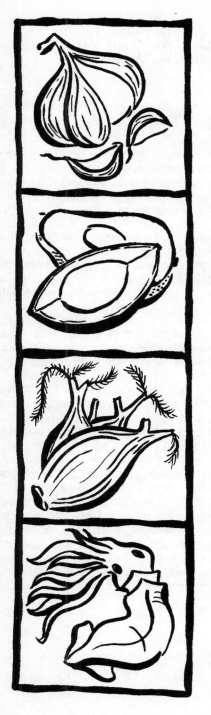

Starters & Snacks

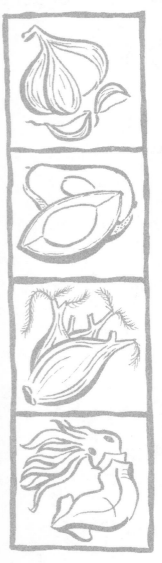

When eating out I often choose two starters rather than a main course because they look so tempting on the menu. No wonder, since starters combine the very best flavours in small amounts, just to tantalize.

When you prepare a small dish, remember that flavour is everything. The taste of the recipe must bounce up and hit you, stimulating the taste buds. Starters need to look good too, so remember to add a garnish with eye-catching colour.

Organic ingredients win here: with their extra-concentrated flavour, you can achieve maximum taste in a minimum amount of food.

I have tried to include a wide range of dishes in this chapter, some that would grace a grand dinner and others with gutsy appeal that are not so elegant. Most of the dishes can be adapted to serve a crowd.

The secret to being able to produce good starters and snacks is to maintain a well-stocked storecupboard, full of the tastiest items, like quality olive and nut oils and fruit vinegars, homemade pesto (see page 30), chopped chilli and the Japanese tamari and miso. You will then find that you can put something small, delicious and imaginative together in a matter of moments.

Mezze

If you have visited Greece or the Middle East, you will have come across mezze, a mixture of many small tasty dishes, anything up to forty at a meal, which are brought to the table a few at a time to tempt the palate.

A mezze always begins with a selection of dips which, together with some good olives and nuts, makes the perfect first course to a meal. Passing the dishes, tasting and dipping, is guaranteed to break the ice among a group of strangers, who will be the best of friends by the time the last dish is empty.

Spiced Nuts

Organic nuts are available from good wholefood shops and organic suppliers. Make sure that they are fresh and full of good nut-oil flavour.

45ml (3 tablespoons) sunflower or safflower oil	large pinch of garam masala powder small pinch of chilli powder
225g (8oz) mixed skinned peanuts, almonds and cashews	pinch of sea salt

- Heat the oil in a large frying pan. Add the nuts and stir constantly for about 3 minutes until they are golden. Remove the nuts from the pan with a slotted spoon and drain them on kitchen paper.

- Sprinkle the nuts with the garam masala, chilli powder and sea salt. Stir well and leave to cool.

- Keep in an airtight tin until ready to serve.

Dips

I often use dips as a delaying food. When the hungry gather in anticipation and dinner is no more than a germinating thought in my mind, I keep the wolves at bay with a bowl of dip and some warm pitta bread.

Cook's Note
When using garlic in an uncooked dish, the flavour can be pungent: it is best to chop the cloves, sprinkle over 2.5ml (½ teaspoon) sea salt, then crush the garlic to a paste with the blade of a knife. This paste spreads its flavour well.

Houmous

A dip made from chickpeas that makes an excellent sandwich filling too.

150g (5oz) dried chickpeas, soaked in cold water overnight	**For the garnish**
	olive oil
2 cloves garlic, crushed with sea salt	paprika
150ml (¼ pint) best-quality olive oil	
60ml (4 tablespoons) fresh lemon juice, or more to taste	
freshly ground black pepper	

- Drain and rinse the soaked chickpeas well, then put them in a pan and cover with water. Boil for about 1¼ hours until they are quite soft.

- Drain the chickpeas and mash them to a paste in a food processor. Add the garlic, olive oil, 60ml (4 tablespoons) lemon juice and black pepper to taste. Blend until smooth and thick. Taste to check that there is enough seasoning, adding more lemon juice and salt if necessary.

- Serve in a bowl, topped with a dribble of olive oil and a sprinkling of paprika.

Tahini

A classic dish from the Middle East, tahini is so versatile that it can be served at the beginning of a meal, as part of a mezze or as a side sauce with both hot and cold dishes. When I see a jar of organic tahini paste on my travels, it is the first item to reach my shopping basket.

60ml (4 tablespoons) tahini paste
2 cloves garlic, crushed with sea salt
juice of 1 large or 2 small lemons
freshly ground black pepper

60ml (4 tablespoons) best-quality
  olive oil
5ml (1 teaspoon) cumin seeds, freshly
  ground in a spice mill
chopped fresh parsley, to garnish

- Put the tahini paste, garlic, lemon juice, pepper, olive oil and ground cumin in a food processor and blend until smooth. The mixture will be very thick, so gradually add 45-60ml (3-4 tablespoons) cold water while blending it in the machine, to thin it to a dipping consistency.
- Serve in a bowl, with a sprinkling of parsley for garnish.

Taramasalata

Homemade taramasalata is quite delicious, a far cry from those pots of pallid pink dip which masquerade under the same name but taste of very little. Originating in the Eastern Mediterranean, it used to be made from tarama, the dried smoked roe of grey mullet but, due to its high price, it has now been replaced by cod's roe.

2 slices of bread, crusts removed
100g (4oz) smoked cod's roe,
  skinned
1 clove garlic, crushed with sea salt
1 shallot or small onion, finely grated
juice of 1-2 lemons

120ml (4½fl oz) best-quality olive oil,
  or more to taste
sea salt and freshly ground black
  pepper
1 slice of lemon, to garnish

- Soak the bread in cold water for 10 minutes to soften, then squeeze dry.
- In a bowl, beat the cod's roe, bread, garlic and shallot together. Add the juice of 1 lemon, then slowly add the olive oil, beating hard to make a smooth sauce. Add salt and pepper, then taste and add more lemon juice and olive oil if you like.
- Serve piled in a bowl, topped with a slice of lemon.

Melitzanosalata

Grilled aubergine has the most wonderful flavour and brings such an exotic richness to this dip that diners find it hugely tempting. In fact, it is said to have been invented by the ladies of the Sultan's harem to win his favours!

2 medium aubergines	30-45ml (2-3 tablespoons) best-
2 cloves garlic, crushed with sea salt	quality olive oil
1 shallot or small onion, grated	sea salt and freshly ground black
juice of 1 small or ½ large lemon	pepper
	chopped fresh coriander, to garnish

- Chop the stalks off the aubergines, then cut the aubergines lengthways in half. Grill them gently, skin side up, for about 15 minutes until the skins begin to char and blister. Don't let them blacken too much.
- Chop the cooked aubergines into chunks and purée with all the other ingredients in a food processor.
- Serve in a bowl, topped with a sprinkling of chopped coriander.

Zatziki

A Greek dish which combines the coolness of yogurt with lovely fresh mint and cucumber.

½ cucumber
150ml (¼ pint) Greek yogurt
½ handful of fresh mint leaves, chopped

sea salt and freshly ground black pepper

- Grate the cucumber and leave it in a sieve or colander to drain for 10 minutes.
- Press the excess juices out and mix the cucumber with the yogurt and chopped fresh mint. Season to taste.

Guacamole

This delicious avocado dip can be prepared as a smooth green purée or a rather chunky dip with tomatoes. For the first, simply mash the avocado with some lemon juice and best mayonnaise and season to taste. If you prefer a textured and spicy guacamole, then here is a recipe.

---

2 ripe avocados
juice of 1 lemon
3 ripe tomatoes
1 clove garlic, crushed with sea salt
4 spring onions, chopped
1 fresh chilli, deseeded and finely
   diced

30ml (2 tablespoons) best-quality
   olive oil
freshly ground black pepper
15ml (1 tablespoon) fresh coriander
   leaves, to garnish

- Peel the avocados, cut them in half lengthways and remove the stones. Dice the flesh and squeeze the lemon juice over it.

- Peel the tomatoes: cover them with boiling water for 15 seconds, then rinse them under the cold tap – the skin should peel off easily. Cut the tomatoes into quarters, scoop out the seeds and discard them. Dice the flesh.

- Mix the diced avocado with the tomatoes, garlic, spring onions, chilli, olive oil and black pepper. Taste for seasoning and add more salt if necessary.

- Spoon into a bowl and scatter over the coriander leaves.

Asparagus with Smoked Salmon and Eggs

This is a great recipe for those skinny asparagus stems or sprue which have a great flavour but aren't fat enough to eat on their own. Mixed with creamy scrambled free-range eggs, the flavour of the asparagus really comes through. As for the salmon, well it just adds a little class.

30ml (2 tablespoons) olive oil	sea salt and freshly ground black
450g (1lb) fresh young asparagus, cut	pepper
into 5cm (2in) lengths	4 slices of best smoked salmon
6 large eggs	4 slices of brioche loaf, toasted
30ml (2 tablespoons) cream or	paprika, to garnish
creamy milk	

- In a large pan, heat the oil and cook the asparagus over medium heat for 2-3 minutes until it begins to colour. Turn the heat down.

- Beat the eggs together with the cream and seasoning and pour the mixture into the pan. Stir continuously as the eggs begin to set, but stop cooking before they set completely.

- Arrange the smoked salmon over the toasted brioche and spoon the asparagus and eggs on top.

- Serve immediately, with a dusting of paprika on the plate.

Potted Trout

An old-fashioned recipe that makes the best of freshly caught trout. Although there is quite a lot of butter, it does make for a good rich flavour, which offsets the muddiness of river or brown trout.

450g (1lb) trout fillets, skin and all bones removed	sea salt and freshly ground black pepper
15ml (1 tablespoon) chopped fresh dill	225g (8oz) slightly salted butter
5ml (1 teaspoon) ground mace	warm fresh toast or Melba toast, to serve

- In a small earthenware pot or terrine, arrange half the trout fillets in one layer. Scatter over the dill, mace and seasoning. Arrange the remaining trout fillets on top.

- In a small pan, gently heat the butter until it melts. Do not let it boil. Pour the melted butter carefully over the trout fillets so they are completely covered, leaving the creamy white sediment from the butter in the bottom of the pan.

- Cover with foil or a lid and bake in a pre-heated moderate oven, 180°C, 350°F, Gas Mark 4, for 20 minutes.

- Remove from the oven and leave to cool completely, then chill in the refrigerator for at least 4 hours for the butter to harden.

- Serve chilled, with warm fresh toast or Melba toast.

Cook's Note
To make Melba toast, toast sliced bread on both sides and, while still warm, slit sideways with a sharp knife to make 2 thin slices. Cut in half diagonally to make triangles, then toast the uncooked sides of bread until crisp.

Bloody Mary Ice in Avocado

Wickedly good fun, this bright red ice makes a great first course for a party on a warm summer's evening. The acidity in the tomatoes, together with the flavours from the basil, spice up the avocado base and create a very exciting taste sensation.

6 large plum tomatoes
2 good sprigs of fresh basil
pinch of sugar
pinch of celery salt
sea salt and freshly ground black
   pepper
5ml (1 teaspoon) Worcestershire
   sauce
5ml (1 teaspoon) fresh lemon juice

To serve
2 avocados
salad
20ml (4 teaspoons) vodka

- Quarter the tomatoes and scoop the seeds and flesh from the middle straight into a sieve. Press hard to extract the juice. In a food processor, blend the quartered tomatoes, the tomato juice and the basil. Add the sugar, celery salt, sea salt, pepper, Worcestershire sauce and lemon juice, then taste and adjust amounts to create a tangy tomato purée.

- Pour into a plastic container, seal with the lid and freeze for at least 6 hours.

- To serve, peel the avocados, cut them in half lengthways and remove the stones. Arrange each avocado half on a bed of salad. Scoop the Bloody Mary ice into ball shapes and sit 1 ball in the stone cavity of each avocado. Drizzle 5ml (1 teaspoon) vodka over each ball of tomato ice and serve immediately, with crisp cheese biscuits.

Brie with Mediterranean Salsa

The combination of Mediterranean flavours brings colour and a taste of the summer to this dish and creates a sharp contrast to the creamy white brie. There is an excellent organic Brie-type cheese made in Wales called Pencarreg which would be great in this recipe. Alternatively, use one you enjoy.

6 firm tomatoes, deseeded and finely diced
100ml (3½fl oz) best-quality olive oil
1 large clove garlic, crushed
20 black olives, stoned and very finely chopped or coarsely ground in a grinder for a few seconds
15ml (1 tablespoon) white wine vinegar
15ml (1 tablespoon) chopped fresh parsley
15ml (1 tablespoon) chopped fresh chives
50g (2oz) can anchovy fillets, drained and chopped
sea salt and freshly ground black pepper
225g (8oz) Brie cheese

- Mix together the tomatoes, olive oil, garlic, olives, wine vinegar, parsley, chives, anchovies and seasoning. Spoon some of this salsa in the middle of each serving plate.

- Slice the cheese as finely as you can without breaking it, then arrange the slices on top of the salsa like the petals of a flower. Sprinkle the remaining salsa around the plates.

- Serve with warm malted bread.

Chicken Satay with Peanut and Coconut Sauce

There is something very appealing about little bamboo sticks of tasty chicken and, although the preparation takes some time, it is well worth the effort. The flavours of the spices, mixed with the sweet soy sauce and sugar, blend to make a good marinade. The flavours of the sauce are lively and hot, but balanced by the cool coconut milk.

4 chicken breasts, skinned

For the marinade
2 cloves garlic, crushed
5ml (1 teaspoon) cardamom seeds, freshly ground in a spice mill
5ml (1 teaspoon) coriander seeds, freshly ground in a spice mill
5ml (1 teaspoon) grated fresh root ginger
grated rind and juice of 1 unwaxed lime
15ml (1 tablespoon) dark soy sauce
5ml (1 teaspoon) muscovado sugar
30ml (2 tablespoons) peanut oil
pinch of sea salt

For the sauce
45ml (3 tablespoons) crunchy peanut butter
1 clove garlic, crushed
1 small fresh red chilli, deseeded and finely chopped, or 5ml (1 teaspoon) chilli sauce
grated rind and juice of 1 unwaxed lime
5ml (1 teaspoon) grated fresh root ginger
15ml (1 tablespoon) soy sauce
50ml (2fl oz) hot water
30ml (2 tablespoons) coconut milk
10ml (2 teaspoons) muscovado sugar, or more to taste
pinch of sea salt, or more to taste

- Soak 12 bamboo satay sticks in cold water for 2 hours.

- Meanwhile, cut the chicken into 2.5cm (1in) cubes and place in a bowl. Mix together all the marinade ingredients, pour over the chicken and turn to coat. Cover and leave to marinate for at least 30 minutes.

- Make the sauce: mix all the ingredients for the sauce together, adding more sugar or sea salt if necessary. Turn into a serving bowl.

- Thread the chicken pieces on the bamboo sticks and grill for about 6 minutes, turning them over once. Serve hot, with the sauce handed separately.

Marinated Salmon with Pesto

This is one of the easiest of fish dishes to prepare and I often serve it to a crowd. Although only a little pesto is used in this recipe, I always make up a large batch and keep it in the refrigerator. There are endless ways of adding a little pesto to so many dishes.

175g (6oz) salmon tail or boneless fillet (wild if possible)

30ml (2 tablespoons) best-quality olive oil

grated rind and juice of 1 unwaxed lime

For the pesto

5 good sprigs of fresh basil (about 30 leaves)

5 good sprigs of fresh flat-leaf parsley (about 30 leaves)

2 cloves garlic, crushed

50g (2oz) pine nuts

45ml (3 tablespoons) best-quality olive oil

sea salt and freshly ground black pepper

- First make the pesto: simply combine all the ingredients in a food processor and whizz until you have a smooth paste.

- Skin the salmon and slice it thinly. Arrange the slices in a shallow dish.

- Mix together the olive oil, lime rind and juice, 5ml (1 teaspoon) pesto, salt and pepper. Pour over the salmon and stir to ensure that all of the fish is well coated. Cover and leave to marinate for at least 2 hours.

- To serve, arrange the salmon slices in a single layer across a white plate and drizzle the pesto around the edge. Serve with lots of fresh bread, to soak up the juices.

Squid in Red Wine with Soba Noodles

It is possible to buy prepared squid, all ready to slice up for this recipe, but I sometimes think that true reward comes to those who prepare this dish from scratch. Japanese soba noodles are available from good health food and organic shops, but any buckwheat noodles would work well.

450g (1lb) prepared squid	1 bay leaf
45ml (3 tablespoons) olive oil	1 cinnamon stick
2 onions, sliced	sea salt and freshly ground black
100ml (3½fl oz) red wine	pepper
200ml (7fl oz) water	100g (4oz) soba buckwheat noodles
15ml (1 tablespoon) sun-dried tomato	chopped fresh parsley, to garnish
paste	

- If the squid has not been prepared, tackle it in the sink with the cold tap running. Pull out the inner contents from the sac, including the stiff clear backbone, and discard. Rinse the squid well, reserving the ink sac if it is still there. Slice the body. Leave the head intact, or snip off the tentacles and reserve them. Squeeze out and discard the beak.

- Heat the oil in a pan and cook the onions gently until soft. Turn up the heat, add the squid and the tentacles and cook briskly until they turn pink. Add the wine, water, tomato paste, bay leaf, cinnamon and seasoning. Cover and simmer for 10 minutes until the squid is tender and the sauce thick.

- Meanwhile, cook the noodles in plenty of salted boiling water for 5-7 minutes until *al dente*. Drain and rinse briefly in cold water to stop them cooking.

- Remove the bay leaf and cinnamon stick from the cooked squid, then add the noodles and mix them well with the sauce.

- Sprinkle with parsley and serve warm or cold, with lots of fresh bread to soak up the sauce.

Smoked Duck with Strawberry Vinaigrette

This is the simplest of dishes, but the ingredients are important. Do try to find naturally smoked duck if you can and make sure that the strawberries are full of flavour, even if they do not look perfect. This recipe works well with smoked chicken or quail too.

15ml (1 tablespoon) sunflower seeds
salad leaves of varying texture and
   colour (eg oak leaf and lamb's
   lettuce)
1 bunch of fresh mixed herbs
2 smoked duck breasts
strawberries, to garnish

For the vinaigrette
100g (4oz) strawberries
60ml (4 tablespoons) best-quality
   olive oil
15ml (1 tablespoon) white wine or
   cider vinegar
sugar or honey, to taste
a little lemon juice (optional)

- First make the vinaigrette: blend or liquidize all the ingredients, then taste and check for balance of flavours, adding sugar or honey and lemon juice to taste.

- Dry-fry the sunflower seeds over medium heat until they begin to turn brown. Pile the salad leaves on individual plates. Chop the fresh herbs and scatter them over the salad with the sunflower seeds.

- Slice the duck breasts and arrange the slices over the salad. Pour some vinaigrette over the duck and garnish with strawberries. Serve the remaining vinaigrette separately.

Crostini

Toasted open sandwiches, Italian crostini make a perfect snack at any time of day, the most wonderful rustic bite to enjoy with a glass of wine. To make good crostini, the bread and its preparation are important. So too is the combination of flavours and colours for the toppings.

The Bread
Well-flavoured 'country' bread is what you need, such as firm-textured rye or mixed grain bread, properly made. Since it is to be toasted, it can be a little on the stale side.

Preparation
Either grill or, better still, griddle on a griddle pan so that attractive stripes appear on the surface of the bread. Some first-pressing virgin olive oil should be drizzled over the bread, then some of the following ingredients arranged on top.

Toppings
- Chopped fresh tomatoes
- Crushed garlic, either raw, sautéed or roasted
- Soft spreading cheese, or firm cheese cut into shavings
- Fresh herbs, whole leaves rather than chopped
- Prawns, tuna, sardines, anchovies
- Charred peppers, sautéed onions or leeks, roasted aubergines
- Grilled bacon, charred chicken breast, slivers of rare venison or beef
- Salami, cured sausages
- Scrambled eggs

Pork with Pak Choi

These pork meatballs take time to prepare, but are well worth the effort, and they make a good starter on their own or as part of a mezze. Pak choi is similar to Chinese cabbage in looks, but with a taste of mustard and pepper and a crisp texture. When cooked, it is a fine green colour. It is now grown organically, but if you have problems finding it or do not grow it yourself, use Chinese cabbage.

60ml (4 tablespoons) sunflower or safflower oil
4 spring onions, sliced
1 clove garlic, crushed
5ml (1 teaspoon) grated fresh root ginger
225g (8oz) pak choi, sliced
15ml (1 tablespoon) tamari or light soy sauce

For the meatballs
450g (1lb) minced pork
1 medium potato, grated
1 shallot or small onion, finely chopped or grated
1 small egg
15ml (1 tablespoon) chopped fresh parsley
2.5ml (½ teaspoon) Chinese five-spice powder
sea salt and freshly ground black pepper

- First make the meatballs: put all the ingredients in a bowl and mix them together, kneading well. Press a crust of bread down on top of the mixture, to absorb any excess moisture, then place the bowl in the refrigerator for at least 30 minutes.

- With damp hands, roll the meat mixture into 2.5cm (1in) balls. Fry them slowly in half the oil for about 10 minutes.

- Meanwhile, heat a wok or frying pan and add the remaining oil. Toss in the spring onions, garlic and ginger and cook for about 30 seconds. Add the pak choi and stir-fry for a couple of minutes until it begins to wilt. Lower the heat, add the tamari and cook for a further minute.

- To serve, mound the pak choi on individual plates and arrange the meatballs on top.

Crispy Thai Prawns

Fresh prawns are readily available these days, so buy them from a reputable fishmonger who can guarantee their freshness. For the sauce, again the freshest of ingredients will create the best flavours and you can make the sauce as hot as you like with the red chilli. Although this dish takes time to prepare – it's worth it!

225g (8oz) uncooked prawns
grated rind and juice of 1 unwaxed lime
1 clove garlic, crushed
5ml (1 teaspoon) grated fresh root ginger
1/2 fresh green chilli, deseeded and finely chopped
15ml (1 tablespoon) light soy sauce
60ml (4 tablespoons) cornflour
75ml (5 tablespoons) breadcrumbs
1 egg, beaten
200ml (7fl oz) sunflower or safflower oil

For the dipping sauce
1 fresh red chilli, deseeded and finely chopped, or 5ml (1 teaspoon) chilli sauce
15ml (1 tablespoon) fish sauce
15ml (1 tablespoon) light soy sauce
juice of 1 lime
5ml (1 teaspoon) sugar
pinch of sea salt
15ml (1 tablespoon) water

- First make the dipping sauce: put all the ingredients in a bowl and mix well together. Set aside.

- Peel the prawns, leaving the tails on. Remove the black digestive cords. Mix the prawns with the lime rind and juice, garlic, ginger, chilli and soy sauce.

- Put the cornflour and breadcrumbs in 2 separate plastic bags. Toss the prawns in the bag of cornflour, then dip them in the beaten egg to cover. Finally, toss them in the bag of breadcrumbs. Put the coated prawns on a plate and leave, uncovered, in the refrigerator for about 15 minutes. This will help to crisp up the coating.

- Heat the oil in a large deep pan or wok. When the oil begins to smoke slightly, deep-fry the coated prawns for 3-4 minutes or until they are golden brown. Drain well on kitchen paper.

- Serve immediately, with the bowl of dipping sauce.

Quiche Lorraine

Quiche Lorraine has been through some sort of metamorphosis since the quote 'real men don't eat quiche'. It seems that both the quiche and real men have survived this challenge. Today you can buy savoury flans of every hue with a varying amount of flavour and texture, but I think that there is little available to beat the classic recipe for bacon and onion in a rich and creamy cheese custard set in good pastry. Especially when the ingredients have been produced organically.

350g (12oz) plain flour
pinch of sea salt
175g (6oz) mixed butter and white
   vegetable fat
a little cold water, to mix

For the filling
100g (4oz) bacon (ideally smoked
   streaky), diced

2 shallots, 1 medium onion or 1
   bunch of spring onions, diced
300ml (½ pint) mixed milk and cream
2 eggs and 2 egg yolks, whisked
   together
100g (4oz) mature Cheddar cheese,
   grated
sea salt and freshly ground black
   pepper

- First make the pastry: tip the flour into a large bowl and add the salt. Cut the fat into cubes and drop them into the flour. Rub the fat into the flour, using your fingertips and lifting the mixture up and away from the bowl (this will help to keep the pastry cool). Alternatively, use a food processor.

- When you have a mixture that looks like breadcrumbs, pour in enough water to amalgamate the pastry to a dough. Knead for 1 minute until it is smooth and even in texture and colour, then set aside.

- Make the filling: dry-fry the diced bacon until the fat runs and the bacon begins to brown and crisp. Add the shallots and cook until soft, then remove from the heat and add the creamy milk, eggs and grated cheese. Stir well and add seasoning to taste.

- Roll out the pastry and use to line a 25-30cm (10-12in) flan dish or tin. Press thick strips of foil around the sides to prevent the pastry collapsing during baking.

- Bake in a pre-heated very hot oven, 230°C, 450°F, Gas Mark 8, for 10 minutes, just to set the pastry. Remove the foil strips and pour in the filling. Reduce the oven temperature to moderately hot, 200°C, 400°F, Gas Mark 6, and bake until firm and golden brown, about 40 minutes.

- Serve warm or cold.

Chargrilled Fennel with Welsh Rarebit

The mild aniseed flavour of fennel goes very well with the tang of a well-made rarebit sauce. The name 'rarebit', sometimes known as 'rabbit', could well have come from a seventeenth-century saying: 'We did not eat of meat, but of Welsh rabbit with cheese.' Once prepared, the rarebit topping can be used for a number of dishes. It makes a great topping for chicken, fish or vegetables.

---

2 bulbs of fennel, thinly sliced
a little sunflower or safflower oil

For the rarebit sauce
25g (1oz) butter
225g (8oz) mature Cheddar cheese, grated
15ml (1 tablespoon) Worcestershire sauce

15ml (1 tablespoon) mild mustard
15ml (1 tablespoon) plain flour
60ml (4 tablespoons) beer
sea salt and freshly ground black pepper
cayenne pepper

- First make the rarebit sauce: melt the butter in a pan and stir in the cheese, Worcestershire sauce, mustard, flour, beer and seasonings so that you have a thick paste. Remove from the heat.

- Heat a grill pan or griddle and brush the slices of fennel lightly with oil. Grill until just beginning to char.

- Arrange the fennel slices in a heatproof dish and spread the Welsh rarebit over them. Grill gently until the mixture bubbles and begins to brown.

- Serve hot.

Eggs Florentine

When I first left home, this is the first dish I remember eating in a restaurant in London. I enjoyed the freedom of the moment and paying the bill for one of the most delicious combinations of flavours I had ever eaten. Today, with the opportunity of wonderful, fresh organic spinach, mature Cheddar cheese and the freshest of eggs, it is a dish that has come into its own again.

4 eggs
900g (2lb) spinach
a few spoonfuls of grated mature
    Cheddar cheese, for the topping

For the cheese sauce
25g (1oz) butter

25g (1oz) plain flour
300ml (½ pint) full-cream milk
50g (2oz) mature Cheddar cheese,
    grated
sea salt and freshly ground black
    pepper
pinch of English mustard powder

- Soft-boil the eggs for 5 minutes. Rinse immediately in cold water, peel and put back into cold water. Alternatively, you can poach the eggs.

- Make the cheese sauce: melt the butter in a saucepan, stir in the flour to make a thin paste, then whisk in the milk. Bring the sauce to the boil, whisking hard until smooth. Add the grated Cheddar, seasoning and mustard. Remove from the heat.

- Wash the spinach in plenty of cold water, removing any tough stalks. Cook it simply in the water it is holding in the leaves. A covered bowl in the microwave is best for this – metal pans tend to set off the acid in the spinach. The spinach will wilt quickly in the heat and needs to be turned well during cooking.

- Arrange the cooked spinach in either 1 large ovenproof dish or 4 individual dishes. Arrange the eggs on the spinach, then top with the cheese sauce followed by the grated Cheddar.

- Bake in a pre-heated very hot oven, 220-230°C, 425-450°F, Gas Mark 7-8, for 10 minutes, or brown under the grill. Serve hot.

Charred Pepper Tartlets

Never one of my favourite raw ingredients because of their indigestibility, peppers have become a firm favourite since I discovered the pleasure of eating them grilled. They take on a smoky sweet flavour which is enhanced when they become slightly charred. Green peppers can still challenge the teeth, however, so I suggest peeling them. These tasty tartlets are ideal for a light lunch, and they travel particularly well if you are planning a picnic.

350g (12oz) plain flour
pinch of sea salt
175g (6oz) mixed butter and white
   vegetable fat
a little cold water, to mix

For the filling
3 peppers (1 green, 1 yellow, 1 red)
30ml (2 tablespoons) olive oil

2 shallots or 1 medium onion, sliced
300ml (½ pint) mixed milk and cream
2 eggs and 2 egg yolks, whisked
   together
100g (4oz) mature Gouda cheese,
   grated
sea salt and freshly ground black
   pepper

- First make the pastry: tip the flour into a large bowl and add the salt. Cut the fat into cubes and drop them into the flour. Rub the fat into the flour, using your fingertips and lifting the mixture up and away from the bowl (this will help to keep the pastry cool). Alternatively, use a food processor.

- When you have a mixture that looks like breadcrumbs, pour in enough water to amalgamate the pastry to a dough. Knead for 1 minute until it is smooth and even in texture and colour, then set aside.

- Make the filling: halve the peppers and remove everything but the outer shell. Put the peppers in the bottom of the grill pan, drizzle over 15ml (1 tablespoon) of the olive oil and grill until the peppers begin to char at the edges. Lower the heat and continue to cook until they are soft. Cool the peppers, remove the skin and cut the flesh into thin slivers.

- Heat the remaining olive oil and cook the shallots very gently for about 10 minutes. They should be very soft, translucent and beginning to turn golden. Mix the peppers and shallots together, then add the creamy milk, eggs and grated cheese. Stir well and add seasoning to taste.

- Roll out the pastry and use to line 24 tartlet tins. Spoon in the filling. Bake the tartlets in a pre-heated hot oven, 220°C, 425°F, Gas Mark 7, until firm and golden brown, about 25 minutes. Serve warm or cold.

Rich Fish Omelette

This is the most wonderful recipe for an omelette, full of flavour, rich and delicious, and has been a favourite since I was at Cordon Bleu College. In those days, smoked haddock was bright yellow and the omelette had a 'high glow' appeal. Today, with naturally smoked fish, the dish looks much more tempting, and with the simple addition of freshly grated Parmesan, the flavours are great.

225g (8oz) naturally smoked (not dyed) haddock 30ml (2 tablespoons) crème fraîche 5 eggs	30-45ml (2-3 tablespoons) freshly grated Parmesan cheese sea salt and freshly ground black pepper 25g (1oz) butter

- Steam or microwave the haddock until just opaque, then flake the flesh, removing the skin and bones. Mix the fish with the crème fraîche.

- Separate the eggs. Beat the yolks together with some salt and pepper. Whisk the egg whites until stiff in a separate clean bowl and fold into the yolks with the haddock and half the Parmesan.

- Heat the butter in an omelette or frying pan. When it stops sizzling, pour in the egg mixture and stir to encourage the omelette to cook evenly. When it begins to set, scatter over the remaining Parmesan. Finish cooking under the grill until set.

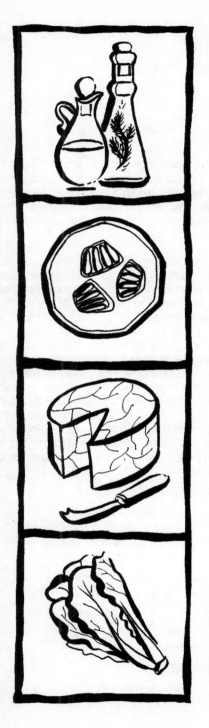

Salads

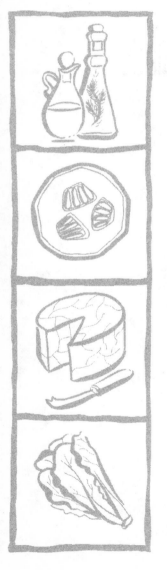

If you are not convinced about organic produce, just see what a difference organic salad ingredients make to a meal. Test the flavour of any of the many lettuces now available, chew on a carrot, crunch a cucumber or munch some herbs.

Growing your own salad vegetables has to be the most satisfying food experience because they can be left in the earth until minutes before a meal, but organic salad stuff is readily available and there is lots to choose from.

Over the past decade, the ingredients for salads have become much more exciting. Long gone are the days of a limp salad containing nothing but lettuce. We think nothing now of adding nuts, croûtons, snippets of meat or fish and delicious cheeses. Dressings, too, are more adventurous. Organic oils, vinegars, mustards and other flavourings ensure that a dressing can add extra taste to any salad you care to create.

Greek Village Salad

Every visitor to Cyprus will come across this delicious local salad. The ingredients and dressing vary a little depending where you eat it on the island, but it is always a good option on the menu, served with fresh village or pitta bread. The fresh herbs and tangy feta cheese give it a truly refreshing taste. Can't you just hear that Greek music now!

1 small white cabbage, shredded
4 spring onions, chopped
1 small or ½ large cucumber, diced
4 juicy red plum tomatoes, quartered
15ml (1 tablespoon) fresh rocket, snipped coarsely with scissors
15ml (1 tablespoon) roughly chopped fresh parsley (flat-leaf if possible)
15ml (1 tablespoon) fresh coriander leaves, snipped coarsely with scissors

50g (2oz) feta cheese, sliced
25-50g (1-2oz) black olives

For the dressing
90ml (3½fl oz) best-quality olive oil
juice of ½ lemon
sea salt and freshly ground black pepper

- Arrange the ingredients in a large salad bowl, starting with the shredded cabbage at the bottom and finishing with the black olives on top.
- Make the dressing: mix the olive oil, lemon juice and seasoning together.
- Pour the dressing over the salad just before serving.

Alfalfa and Chickpea Salad with Ginger and Sesame Dressing

A healthy salad full of crunchy ingredients and, for those who sprout their own seeds, a sense of satisfaction. Commercial sprouters are readily available and alfalfa seeds take 3-4 days, growing to a height of 2.5-5cm. Do not forget to grow them in a warm place and keep the sprouts well drained, otherwise they will rot. The oriental dressing adds to the flavour to make this a most rewarding salad to prepare.

50g (2oz) dried chickpeas, soaked in cold water overnight, or 1/2 x 425g (15oz) can chickpeas, drained and rinsed
225g (8oz) beansprouts
3 peppers (1 red, 1 green, 1 yellow), chopped
1 punnet of alfalfa sprouts
30ml (2 tablespoons) finely chopped fresh parsley

For the dressing
45ml (3 tablespoons) sunflower or safflower oil
5ml (1 teaspoon) sesame oil
5mm (¼in) piece of fresh root ginger, grated
1 clove garlic, crushed
15ml (1 tablespoon) balsamic vinegar

- If using dried chickpeas, drain them and put them in a pan with fresh water. Boil gently for about 1¼ hours. Drain and rinse under the cold tap.

- Pick over the beansprouts and discard any that are not crisp. Put the beansprouts in a large salad bowl and add the chickpeas, peppers, alfalfa and parsley.

- Just before serving, mix together all the ingredients for the dressing and pour over the salad.

Cracked Wheat and Herb Salad

Similar to the Arabic tabbouleh, this must be the simplest and quickest of grain salads to rustle up and, with the predominant flavours of lemon and parsley, it is very refreshing. Cracked wheat, also known as bulgur wheat or pourgouri, is already cooked, so it needs a minimum of preparation. If possible, make it ahead of time, to allow the flavours to develop.

100g (4oz) cracked wheat
30ml (2 tablespoons) finely chopped
fresh flat-leaf parsley
15ml (1 tablespoon) finely chopped
fresh mint
6 spring onions, finely chopped

225g (8oz) firm red tomatoes, finely
chopped
juice of 1 large juicy lemon
45ml (3 tablespoons) best-quality
olive oil
sea salt and freshly ground black
pepper

- Cover the cracked wheat with cold water and leave to stand for 20 minutes, during which time it will swell and become soft and edible. Turn into a sieve and press out all of the water.

- Combine the remaining ingredients in a large salad bowl and stir in the cracked wheat. Season to taste. Cover and leave in the refrigerator for at least 1 hour, preferably overnight.

Spinach, Avocado and Bacon Salad

This salad is an all-time favourite of mine with its great flavours and textures. The rich, creamy avocado and crisp bacon are just saved from seeming too indulgent by the crunchy fresh spinach and spring onions.

100g (4oz) smoked streaky bacon
450g (1lb) fresh spinach, well washed
2 avocados
1 bunch of watercress
4 spring onions, finely chopped

For the dressing
90ml (3½fl oz) best-quality olive oil
30ml (2 tablespoons) raspberry or red
   wine vinegar
15ml (1 tablespoon) runny honey
a handful of fresh herbs
sea salt and freshly ground black
   pepper

- Derind the bacon and snip it into small pieces. Dry-fry it gently in a pan until the fat begins to run, then turn up the heat and cook until very crisp. Remove from the heat.

- If the spinach leaves are large, tear them in half, then arrange them in a large bowl. Peel the avocados, cut them in half lengthways and remove the stones. Dice the flesh. Scatter the watercress, spring onions, avocado and bacon on top of the spinach.

- Mix the ingredients for the dressing together and pour over the salad. Toss well to cover all the ingredients in the dressing.

Latticed Tuna and Anchovy Salad

This is a variation of Salade Niçoise, the classic summer salad from Nice in the south of France. The ingredients are arranged over a wide platter for eye appeal. A warm crusty loaf of bread is good for mopping up the vinaigrette.

350g (12oz) French beans, trimmed 1 cucumber 450g (1lb) plum tomatoes 50g (2oz) can anchovies, drained about 60ml (4 tablespoons) milk 185g (6oz) can tuna in brine or oil, drained 50g (2oz) black olives (the best you can buy)	**For the vinaigrette** 6 tablespoons best-quality olive oil 30ml (2 tablespoons) wine vinegar sea salt and freshly ground black pepper a drop of honey 15ml (1 tablespoon) chopped fresh marjoram

- Blanch the beans in boiling water, then rinse them under the cold tap to retain their colour. Peel the cucumber. Slice half, then cube the other half.

- Peel the tomatoes: cover them with boiling water for 15 seconds, then rinse them under the cold tap – the skin should peel off easily. Slice half the tomatoes and cut the remainder into quarters.

- Soak the anchovy fillets in the milk to reduce the salt. Drain and split them in half lengthways.

- Make the vinaigrette with the oil, vinegar, seasoning, honey and marjoram.

- Arrange the ingredients on a large platter, adding vinaigrette with each layer. Begin with the beans on the bottom, cover with the tuna and cubed cucumber and then the sliced tomatoes. Cover everything with sliced cucumber. Make a lattice effect with the anchovies, dot the squares with the olives and arrange the tomato quarters around the edge. Pour over more vinaigrette.

- Serve well chilled.

Sweet Beetroot Salad

Organic beetroot and carrots have the most marvellous flavour and, combined with the richness of balsamic vinegar, make a truly great salad. The colours are superb too. It is well worth paying the price for authentic balsamic vinegar, for its quality of flavour.

225g (8oz) raw beetroot
225g (8oz) carrots

For the dressing
30ml (2 tablespoons) balsamic
    vinegar
75ml (3fl oz) best-quality olive oil
sea salt and freshly ground black
    pepper

- Boil the beetroot in their skins until tender. (A glass dish in the microwave does this most satisfactorily.) Cool, peel and chop the cooked beetroot.

- Peel the carrots if necessary, then grate them.

- Combine the beetroot and carrots in a pretty dish.

- Mix the ingredients for the dressing together and pour over the salad.

Broad Beans and Bacon with Nut Dressing

The first bowl of tender young broad beans from the garden is heaven. However, as the crop continues, it's nice to add some extra flavours, so here is a salad for broad beans with bacon.

450g (1lb) fresh broad beans, shelled
100g (4oz) smoked streaky bacon
100g (4oz) mushrooms (field if
   possible)
finely chopped fresh herbs, to garnish

For the dressing
30ml (2 tablespoons) hazelnut or
   walnut oil
juice of ½ lemon
sea salt and freshly ground black
   pepper

- Steam the beans for 5-6 minutes, then rinse them immediately under the cold tap to retain their bright green colour.
- Derind the bacon and snip it into small pieces. Dry-fry it gently in a pan until the fat begins to run, then turn up the heat and cook until very crisp. Remove from the heat.
- Trim the mushroom stalks and cut the mushrooms lengthways.
- Toss the beans, bacon and mushrooms together in a serving bowl. Blend the dressing ingredients together, pour over the salad and garnish with chopped fresh herbs.

Three Lettuce Salad

I think that the best green salads are made from as many different lettuces and herbs as you can grow or find. With a mixture of texture, flavour and colours there is nothing to beat a well-dressed green salad as a first course or accompaniment to almost any dish.

1 crisp lettuce (eg Webb)	**For the dressing**
1 red lettuce (eg oak leaf)	45ml (3 tablespoons) best-quality
1 frisée	olive oil
a selection of small leaves (eg lamb's	15ml (1 tablespoon) cider or white
lettuce, endive, dandelion)	wine vinegar
1 bunch of watercress	¼ teaspoon honey
45ml (3 tablespoons) chopped fresh	¼ teaspoon wholegrain mustard
herbs (eg chives, parsley, golden	sea salt and freshly ground black
marjoram, fennel, basil)	pepper
nasturtium leaves and flowers, to	
garnish	

- Wash all the lettuces in lots of cold water.

- Spin to dry and arrange in manageable-sized pieces in the largest of salad bowls. Scatter over the smaller salad leaves, watercress and herbs.

- Mix all the ingredients together for the dressing, pour over the salad and toss very, very well. Garnish with nasturtium leaves and flowers before serving.

Marinated Grilled Vegetables

This is a seriously good way of serving Mediterranean vegetables. They are perfect on their own or as an accompaniment to another dish, such as baked sea bass in salt or anything coming off the barbecue.

3 large fleshy peppers (different colours), cut into slivers
1 medium aubergine, cut lengthways into thin strips
2 medium courgettes, sliced across at an angle
1 mild red onion, sliced
2 cloves garlic, halved
olive oil, for brushing
4 flat field mushrooms

For the dressing
90ml (3½fl oz) best-quality olive oil
30ml (2 tablespoons) red wine vinegar
1 clove garlic, crushed
chopped fresh herbs, to taste
sea salt and freshly ground black pepper

- In a roasting tin, arrange the peppers, aubergine, courgettes, onion and garlic in a single layer and brush with olive oil. Grill or bake in a pre-heated hot oven, 220°C, 425°F, Gas Mark 7, until they soften in the middle and begin to char at the edges.

- Brush the mushrooms with olive oil, add to the tin and cook for a further 10 minutes.

- Discard the garlic and arrange the rest of the vegetables in a dish. Mix the dressing ingredients together and pour over the vegetables. Leave to marinate for at least 30 minutes.

- Serve with lots of fresh bread to soak up the juices.

Potato Salad with Yogurt Dressing

A good potato salad is a very comforting dish. Search out well-flavoured, waxy potatoes – little new potatoes work particularly well. Add some extra fresh herbs if you wish, but always have an element of onion with the potatoes, such as chives or chopped shallot. The dressing here is light and tangy, and it makes a pleasant change from mayonnaise.

900g (2lb) waxy potatoes
1 bunch of fresh chives, chopped

For the dressing
60ml (4 tablespoons) Greek yogurt or
   fromage frais

5ml (1 teaspoon) wholegrain mustard
juice of ½ lemon
15ml (1 tablespoon) cider vinegar
sea salt and freshly ground black
   pepper

- Boil or, better still, steam the potatoes in their skins.

- Mix the yogurt, mustard, lemon juice and vinegar together and season to taste.

- Chop the potatoes into bite-sized pieces while they are still warm and put them in a serving dish. Immediately pour the dressing over them and scatter the chives on top.

Chargrilled Chicken Salad

Chicken with lots of flavour is essential for this, so try to find one that has been organically reared and hung well. This salad can be a first course or a complete meal when served with some good bread. The dressing is enriched with a raw egg. It can be omitted if you prefer.

2 chicken breasts
olive oil, for brushing
100g (4oz) lean bacon, cubed
15ml (1 tablespoon) pine nuts
1 large Cos lettuce
1 large avocado
25g (1oz) fresh Parmesan cheese

For the croûtons
15ml (1 tablespoon) sunflower or
    safflower oil
1 clove garlic

2 slices of bread, crusts removed and
    cubed

For the dressing
75ml (3fl oz) best-quality olive oil
juice of 1 lemon
1 raw egg
15ml (1 tablespoon) Worcestershire
    sauce
sea salt and freshly ground black
    pepper

- Skin the chicken breasts and split them across so that you have 4 thin escalopes. Brush them with oil and grill, griddle or pan-fry gently so that they cook through. Turn up the heat to brown and crisp the surface, then remove them from the pan and cut them into strips.

- Dry-fry the bacon cubes until they are crisp. Dry-fry the pine nuts until they brown.

- Make the croûtons: heat the oil and fry the whole garlic clove gently for a few minutes, then add the cubes of bread and fry until crisp. Remove from the heat and discard the garlic.

- Mix all the ingredients together for the dressing. Arrange some of the lettuce leaves around the sides of a salad bowl. Tear the rest into smaller, more manageable-sized pieces and toss with the dressing, then fill in the centre of the bowl.

- Peel the avocado, cut it in half lengthways and remove the stone. Dice the flesh and scatter it over the salad with the chicken, bacon, pine nuts and croûtons. Finally, add shavings of fresh Parmesan on top.

Pressed Tapenade and French Bread Salad

This is a favourite family dish which reminds us of the holidays in Provence when we used to make it every evening after supper. Using the best of the salad ingredients left at the end of the day and the remaining French bread, we collected all the best flavours we could find in the kitchen and filled them into the split loaf. By pressing the baguette overnight, the flavours would sink into the bread and this economical sandwich made the perfect lunch for us at the local swimming pool the following day. Tapenade, the Provençal olive and anchovy paste, is packed with flavour and gives this salad lots of gusto. You could use other flavours too, from crushed garlic to sardines, and don't forget a good few sprigs of fresh herbs.

- Split a French stick lengthways and spread one half with a thick layer of tapenade.
- Add some extra flavours like sliced onion, sliced tomatoes or tasty cheese.
- Top with some prepared salad, dressing and all.
- Press the lid down hard. Wrap in foil and press the loaf under a weight overnight.
- The next day, slice thinly and serve as an appetizer or picnic treat.

Rocket and Pine Nut Salad

I first came across rocket in Cyprus, where it is used as a salad ingredient all the time. To begin with I found it strong and very peppery, but rocket is addictive and now I love its fiery flavour. The pine nuts, with their sweetness, go well with rocket.

225g (8oz) rocket leaves	5ml (1 teaspoon) runny honey
50g (2oz) pine nuts	60ml (4 tablespoons) hazelnut oil or best-quality olive oil
For the dressing	15ml (1 tablespoon) white wine vinegar
1 small clove garlic, crushed	
2.5ml (½ teaspoon) wholegrain mustard	sea salt and freshly ground black pepper

- Arrange the clean rocket leaves in a salad bowl.

- Toast the pine nuts until they begin to brown, either under the grill or in a dry pan. Leave the nuts to cool, then sprinkle over the salad.

- Combine the ingredients for the dressing, pour over the salad and toss well.

- Soups
- Starters & Snacks
- Salads
- Vegetarian
- Fish
- Meat
- Poultry & Game
- Baking
- Desserts

Vegetarian

Absolutely fabulous, the only words to describe the amount of flavour you can pack into vegetarian dishes based on organic ingredients. This is the largest section in the book, simply because there are so many ingredients to choose from and therefore a host of delicious dishes to be created.

Starting with vegetables, the selection covers root vegetables, greens, Mediterranean or simply fresh garden vegetables. Pulses, pasta, rice, nuts grains, sprouting seeds, even flowers – the list of ingredients is endless. Of course, there are also the soya-based products such as tofu and tempeh and fungus-based products like Quorn, as well as various fresh and dried seaweeds to create dishes with. And that is before we incorporate dairy ingredients: any of the superb organic cheeses available, yogurt, crème frâiche or just good butter.

Styles of cooking are many too, with stir-fry, bake, steam, roast, poach, even microwave.

I hope you join me in my enthusiasm for this selection of vegetarian dishes based on the very best organic produce. You don't have to be vegetarian to enjoy them!

Deep-Fried Garden Vegetables with Japanese Dipping Sauce

This is an adaptation of a tempura recipe, the classic Japanese dish of deep-fried vegetables or fish in a light, lacy batter. Deep-frying as a cooking technique is excellent because of its speed, which seals in the flavour and cooks so fast that no nutrients are lost. The secret of the lovely light batter is to prepare it right at the last minute. The ingredients for the sauce should be available from a good health food shop.

red or green peppers
courgettes
aubergines
shallots
broccoli
cauliflower
button mushrooms
French beans
nori seaweed
vegetable oil, for deep-frying
5ml (1 teaspoon) sesame oil
plain flour, for dusting

For the dipping sauce
150ml (¼ pint) dashi (Japanese stock)
  or vegetable stock
30ml (2 tablespoons) soy sauce
30ml (2 tablespoons) mirin (Japanese
  rice wine) or sweet sherry

For the condiments
2.5cm (1in) piece of fresh root ginger,
  peeled and finely grated
½ daikon radish, peeled and finely
  grated

For the batter
2 egg yolks
475ml (16fl oz) iced water
225g (8oz) plain flour

- Deseed the peppers and cut them into strips. Thinly slice the courgettes and aubergines. Cut the shallots into quarters. Divide the broccoli and cauliflower into florets. Leave the mushrooms whole. Tie the French beans into bundles with strips of seaweed. For 4 people, you should have about 1kg (2¼lb) prepared vegetables, and they should all be in similar-sized pieces.

- Make up the dipping sauce by heating the dashi and adding the other ingredients.

- Arrange the condiments in small bowls to pass around.

- Pour enough vegetable oil into a small saucepan to fill it to a depth of about 5cm (2in). Add the sesame oil and heat to 175°C (340°F).

- Make the batter at the last minute: stir together the egg yolks and iced water with a fork or chopsticks. Add the flour all at once and mix lightly. Don't try to break up all the lumps of flour.

- Toss the vegetables in flour, dip into the batter, then straight into the hot oil. Cook for 1-3 minutes, turning from time to time. Drain on kitchen paper.

- Serve as soon as possible, with the dipping sauce and condiments.

Herb Potato Rösti

Originally from Switzerland, this cake of grated potato, fried until crisp, is served simply with bacon and eggs as a filling and satisfying meal for hungry skiers. It has become something of a celebrity dish recently since chefs discovered that a small rösti makes a fine base for all sorts of sophisticated meat dishes. I find that rösti makes a quick and delicious family supper dish, especially when made with full-flavoured organic potatoes. Only prepare the rösti just before you want to cook it because it is the starch in the freshly grated potatoes that keeps the cake together.

450g (1lb) potatoes (waxy if possible)	sea salt and freshly ground black
1 medium onion, grated	pepper
1 clove garlic, crushed	30ml (2 tablespoons) sunflower or
30ml (2 tablespoons) chopped fresh	safflower oil
herbs	25g (1oz) butter

● Peel the potatoes and grate them coarsely into a bowl. Immediately mix in the onion, garlic, herbs and lots of seasoning. Shape into 1 large cake or 4 small cakes.

● In a large, heavy-based frying pan, heat the oil and butter and add the rösti. As it begins to cook, press it down gently to compress it. Fry gently for at least 5 minutes, then turn the cake over and cook for a further 5 minutes.

● Slide the rösti onto a serving dish and cut into wedges to serve.

Wild Mushroom Risotto

Organic risotto rice is available with the husks on as brown rice, or without the husks as white rice. The recipe for this risotto is based on white rice, but if you prefer to use brown, adapt the amount of stock and lengthen the cooking time to suit. Good mushrooms to mix are shiitake, chanterelles, wood bluettes, trompettes de mort, oysters and button.

75g (3oz) unsalted butter
1 onion, finely chopped
225g (8oz) wild or cultivated
    mushrooms (or a mixture of both),
    sliced
2 cloves garlic, crushed
500g (1lb 2oz) risotto rice

1.7 litres (3 pints) vegetable or
    chicken stock, kept just below
    boiling point
sea salt and freshly ground black
    pepper
50g (2oz) Parmesan cheese, freshly
    grated
6 spring onions, chopped

- Melt 50g (2oz) of the butter in a large, heavy-based saucepan and cook the onion gently until it is soft but not brown. Add 175g (6oz) of the mushrooms and the garlic and cook for 1 minute. Stir in the rice and continue to cook until the grains have become translucent and glossy.

- Add a ladleful of hot stock and stir well, then gradually add the rest of the stock, ladle by ladle, as the rice swells and absorbs it. Stir all the time. This should take about 20-25 minutes.

- With the last ladleful of stock, add salt and pepper to taste and the Parmesan. Take the pan off the heat, cover and leave to stand.

- Melt the remaining butter in a small pan, add the remaining mushrooms and the spring onions and toss together.

- Transfer the risotto to a warmed platter and scatter the extra mushrooms and spring onions over the top.

Spanakopitta

A classic dish from Greece – thin sheets of crisp filo pastry layered with spinach and tangy feta cheese. Make a large dish of spanakopitta so that it can be served hot and then cold afterwards. I haven't found a supply of organic filo pastry yet so, for the purist, I suggest that you make up some pastry and use it as a crust. Cooking spinach in aluminium often gives it a metallic flavour: use cast iron, non-stick or glass for preference.

45ml (3 tablespoons) olive oil	30ml (2 tablespoons) chopped fresh
12 spring onions, finely chopped	parsley
1kg (2¼lb) spinach, chopped and	good pinch of freshly grated nutmeg
washed	100g (4oz) feta cheese, crumbled
sea salt and freshly ground black	2 large or 3 medium eggs, beaten
pepper	about 50g (2oz) butter
	275g (10oz) filo pastry sheets

- Heat the oil and fry the spring onions gently without browning for a few minutes. Add the drained spinach and toss until it begins to wilt. Cover and cook gently for 5 minutes. Alternatively, put the onions and spinach in a covered dish with 30ml (2 tablespoons) water and microwave on High for 5 minutes.

- Allow the spinach to cool a little before adding salt, pepper, parsley, nutmeg, cheese and the beaten eggs.

- Melt the butter and brush some over the bottom of a large, deep, square baking tin or ovenproof dish. Spread 4-5 sheets of filo pastry over the bottom, brushing between each layer with melted butter. Spoon the spinach filling over the filo sheets, then cover with the remaining filo, brushing each sheet with melted butter as before. Tuck the sides under neatly and brush butter over the top of the pie.

- Bake the spanakopitta in a pre-heated moderately hot oven, 200°C, 400°F, Gas Mark 6, for 30-40 minutes, then increase the heat for another 5 minutes to brown the top.

- Serve warm or cold.

Potato Wedges

Rather like homemade chips, these potato wedges are one of the most delicious ways of serving potatoes. They are easy to make, healthy due to lack of oil in the cooking, and full of flavour – especially if you add fresh herbs and a touch of garlic. They also make the best use of maincrop organic potatoes throughout the year.

900g (2lb) medium potatoes
1 tablespoon sunflower or safflower
  oil
sea salt and freshly ground black
  pepper

For the flavourings (optional)
1 clove garlic, crushed
15ml (1 tablespoon) chopped fresh
  herbs
2.5ml (½ teaspoon) cayenne pepper
pinch of curry powder

● Cut the unpeeled potatoes in half, then into wedges, so that each piece has a good edge of skin and they are all about the same size. Put all the wedges in a plastic bag with the oil and salt and pepper.

● Add flavourings of your choice, then shake the bag well so that the potatoes are evenly covered with oil and seasoning.

● Arrange the wedges in a single layer over 1-2 baking trays. Bake in a pre-heated hot oven, 220°C, 425°F, Gas Mark 7, for 20 minutes. Turn the wedges over and return to the oven for another 10 minutes.

● Eat as soon as they come out of the oven.

Couscous with Mediterranean Vegetables

A simple and satisfying dish, using the best of the summer vegetables and an easy grain such as couscous to add bulk and texture. I remember first eating couscous at a campsite in France. It was a great favourite with the French families and you could see the preparations for the meal going on for hours. It was vital to own a couscousier. Happily couscous is now available ready-cooked and it takes only a matter of minutes to prepare in either a steamer or in the microwave.

1 aubergine, cut into chunks
2-3 peppers (red and yellow for preference), deseeded and sliced
3 courgettes, sliced
1 large onion, sliced
2 cloves garlic, crushed
2 fresh green chillies, deseeded and finely chopped
30-45ml (2-3 tablespoons) olive oil

2 x 425g (15oz) cans tomatoes, roughly chopped
1.25ml (¼ teaspoon) harissa, or a mixture of cayenne pepper and paprika
450g (1lb) instant couscous
lots of chopped fresh coriander or parsley, to garnish

- Griddle or grill the aubergine, peppers and courgettes quickly until they begin to char and blister.

- In a large pan, sweat the onion, garlic and chillies gently in the olive oil until soft. Add the grilled vegetables, the tomatoes and harissa. Cover and cook gently for 15 minutes.

- Soak, then steam or microwave the couscous as directed on the packet.

- Serve the couscous piled on a warm serving dish with the vegetables on top. Garnish with lots of freshly chopped coriander or parsley.

Felafel

These crisp little chickpea fritters are found all over the Middle East. They are served in a pitta pocket, which is then filled with a selection of salads and some dressing such as houmous or tahini. Quite delicious, they make the perfect snack.

100g (4oz) dried chickpeas, soaked in
  cold water overnight
1 small onion, chopped
1 clove garlic, chopped
a handful of fresh parsley
2.5ml (½ teaspoon) cumin seeds,
  freshly ground in a spice mill

2.5ml (½ teaspoon) coriander seeds,
  freshly ground in a spice mill
pinch of baking powder
sea salt and freshly ground black
  pepper
sunflower or safflower oil, for frying

- Drain the chickpeas and blend them in a food processor or liquidizer with the onion, garlic, parsley and 30ml (2 tablespoons) water. Add the cumin, coriander, baking powder and seasoning. Chill in the refrigerator for 1 hour.

- Shape the mixture into walnut-sized balls and flatten them slightly. Shallow-fry or deep-fry in hot oil until brown and crisp.

- Serve in pitta bread envelopes with salad and sauces.

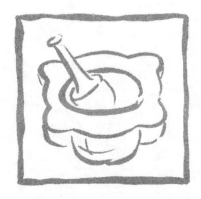

Cypriot Raisin Pilaff

This nutty pilaff of cracked wheat is always served with a bowl of thick Greek yogurt and a wedge of fresh lemon. In Cyprus, cracked wheat or bulgur wheat is known as pourgouri and is something of a staple ingredient, eaten much more than rice or pasta. The grain has already been cooked, so this is a very quick dish to make.

30ml (2 tablespoons) olive oil	300ml (½ pint) good vegetable stock
1 medium onion, finely sliced	50g (2oz) raisins
25g (1oz) vermicelli	sea salt and freshly ground black
225g (8oz) bulgur or cracked wheat	pepper

• Heat the oil in a heavy-based, flameproof casserole and cook the onion gently for 5 minutes. Add the vermicelli, breaking it into the pan with your hands into manageable-sized pieces. Stir for 1 minute until it becomes translucent from absorbing the oil.

• Rinse the wheat under the cold tap, then add to the casserole immediately. Add the stock, raisins and seasoning. Cover and simmer gently for 9-10 minutes or until all the stock is absorbed.

• Leave the pilaff to stand for 5 minutes before serving.

Simple Sicilian Pasta

This must be one of the simplest ways of serving pasta. The recipe was given to my by Mr Piazza, who runs the best Italian deli cum corner shop in town. He insists that it is a failsafe way of packing flavour into a quick dish with a minimum of effort, and I must say I think he is right. A wholewheat pasta works well with this sauce too.

450g (1lb) penne or fusilli	15ml (1 tablespoon) balsamic vinegar
sea salt and freshly ground black pepper	leaves from 1 good sprig of fresh thyme
45ml (3 tablespoons) olive oil	lots of freshly grated Parmesan cheese, to serve
3 cloves garlic, finely sliced	
6 firm tomatoes or 1 x 425g (15oz) can tomatoes	

- Cook the pasta in plenty of salted boiling water according to packet instructions, until *al dente*.

- Meanwhile, heat the oil in a pan and add the garlic. Cook very, very gently for about 10 minutes so that the garlic caramelizes naturally and turns a delicious golden brown.

- If using fresh tomatoes, pour boiling water over them and count to ten. Rinse under the cold tap, then peel away the skin. Roughly chop the tomatoes (fresh or canned) and add to the garlic. Cook for 10 minutes until the tomatoes are completely broken down. Add the balsamic vinegar, thyme leaves and lots of seasoning.

- Drain the pasta and serve with the sauce and lots of freshly grated Parmesan.

Broccoli and Blue Cheese Soufflés

The French word *soufflé* means 'breath of air', and that is why it is important to make light soufflés that literally melt away in the mouth. Making soufflés is a great deal easier than you think, but getting a good flavour into them takes more effort. Any green vegetable makes a good soufflé, but broccoli is particularly successful because the strong flavour blends so well with cheese.

This recipe is for little individual soufflés, but the mixture works well for one large dish – simply allow an extra 10 minutes cooking time.

50g (2oz) butter, plus extra for greasing
a few spoonfuls of dried breadcrumbs
450g (1lb) broccoli, divided into florets
50g (2oz) plain flour
150ml (¼ pint) milk

100g (4oz) strong blue cheese (eg Danish Blue rather than Cambozola), diced or crumbled
4 egg yolks
mustard, to taste
sea salt and freshly ground black pepper
6 egg whites

- Pre-heat the oven to hot, 220°C, 425°F, Gas Mark 7. Grease the insides of 4-6 individual soufflé dishes with a little butter and dust with dried breadcrumbs.

- Blanch the broccoli in a minimum of water until just tender. Retain 65ml (2½fl oz) of the cooking liquid. Purée the cooked broccoli in a food processor or liquidizer.

- Melt the 50g (2oz) butter in a saucepan. Add the flour and cook for 1 minute, stirring to prevent burning. Gradually stir in the milk and the measured broccoli cooking liquid and bring to the boil to thicken. Remove the sauce from the heat and add the cheese, egg yolks, mustard, seasoning and puréed broccoli.

- In a clean bowl, whisk the egg whites until stiff. Fold them into the broccoli mixture, then spoon into the prepared dishes. Bake in the pre-heated oven for 15 minutes until well risen and golden brown.

- Serve immediately.

Polenta with Aubergine and Tomato

I first ate polenta at The Walnut Tree Inn, where Franco Taruschio showed me that it was not difficult to prepare instant polenta. With its grainy texture and pleasant 'cornmeal' flavour, organic polenta is well worth searching out.

1 large or 2 medium aubergines	coarse sea sea salt and freshly
6 large or 8 smaller ripe tomatoes	ground black pepper
1 onion	1 litre (1¾ pints) water
2 cloves garlic	250g (9oz) instant polenta
100ml (4fl oz) olive oil	sprig of fresh herbs, to garnish

- Slice the aubergines, tomatoes, onion and garlic into wedges, like the segments of an orange. Arrange them in a single layer over a large baking tray, spoon over 5 tablespoons of the olive oil and sprinkle with salt and pepper.

- Bake in a pre-heated hot oven, 220°C, 425°F, Gas Mark 7, for about 30 minutes, turning the vegetables from time to time. They are ready when the edges begin to char – you may need to remove the garlic earlier because it browns very quickly.

- For the polenta, bring the water to the boil in a pan, add salt and then the polenta, stirring constantly until you have a firm paste. Remove from the heat, let stand for 1 minute, then turn out onto an oiled plate. Leave to cool.

- When the polenta is cool, cut it into wedges or triangles and fry gently in the remaining olive oil until crisp and golden.

- Serve the polenta wedges with the roasted vegetables piled on top, garnished with a sprig of fresh herbs.

Tofu with Water Chestnuts

This is a recipe for a stir-fry using any of the non-meat protein products such as Quorn, tempeh or tofu. Quorn is made from a cultivated fungus, like a mushroom, and tempeh and tofu are made from soya beans. Choose cubes for their texture. These products are available from a variety of sources but I get my tempeh from a friend in West Wales who is known affectionately as Tom Soya!

45ml (3 tablespoons) dark soy sauce
30ml (2 tablespoons) dry sherry
250g (9oz) tofu, cubed
30ml (2 tablespoons) vegetable oil
1 leek, sliced
1 clove garlic, crushed
a good knob of fresh root ginger, grated
2.5ml (½ teaspoon) Chinese five-spice powder

½ each red, green and yellow pepper, deseeded and sliced
50g (2oz) canned water chestnuts, sliced
250g (9 oz) beansprouts
15ml (1 tablespoon) cornflour blended with 45ml (3 tablespoons) cold water

---

- Mix the soy sauce and sherry together, stir in the tofu and leave to marinate for 30 minutes.

- Heat the oil in a large frying pan or wok and stir-fry the leek, garlic, ginger and spice for 2 minutes. Add the peppers and stir-fry for 2-3 minutes, then mix in the water chestnuts and beansprouts, and the tofu and its marinade. Cook for another few minutes, then add the blended cornflour and stir until the mixture thickens.

- Serve immediately, with Chinese noodles.

Seaweed and Orange Bocconcini

Laver, or *Porphyra umbilicalis*, is used in Wales to make these delicious nutty patties. Japanese nori, which is the same seaweed but dried and pressed, is equally good.

Traditionally, these laverbread cakes were eaten by miners, whose knowing wives served the nutritious laver seaweed to improve their health. As then, it is still fried in bacon fat and served as part of a Welsh breakfast.

100g (4oz) pulped laverbread (available from fishmongers or in a can)
60ml (4 tablespoons) medium-ground oatmeal

grated rind and juice of ½ unwaxed orange (optional)
freshly ground black pepper
15ml (1 tablespoon) sunflower or safflower oil
25g (1oz) butter

- Mix the laverbread with the oatmeal and seasonings. Shape into bocconcini about the size of a large walnut.
- Heat the oil and butter in a frying pan and fry the bocconcini gently until cooked through.

Potato and Fennel Boulangère

Warm and comforting, a spoonful of creamy potato boulangère satisfies all those cold-weather cravings and, with the gentle aniseed flavour of the fennel, this is an all-time winner. It is easy too, since once the potatoes and fennel are sliced, and the dish is in the oven, the cook can take time over the rest of the meal.

4 large potatoes, scrubbed but not peeled	sea salt and freshly ground black pepper
1 bulb of fennel	300ml (½ pint) single cream
butter, for greasing	300ml (½ pint) milk
2 cloves garlic, crushed	1 egg (optional)
	freshly grated nutmeg, to taste

- Slice the potatoes and fennel thinly. Butter a large baking dish and arrange the potato and fennel slices in alternate layers with the garlic and lots of seasoning in between.

- Mix the cream and milk with the egg (if using), the nutmeg and lots of seasoning. Pour this mixture over the vegetables. Cover with foil and bake in a pre-heated moderately hot oven, 190°C, 375°F, Gas Mark 5, for at least 1½ hours, removing the foil for the last 30 minutes to brown the top.

Sesame Seed Stir-fry

The flavour of mushrooms and beansprouts is greatly enhanced by the addition of sesame oil. Just add it at the last minute and it will also bring out the flavour of the toasted sesame seeds, adding something special to this simple stir-fry.

30ml (2 tablespoons) olive oil	15ml (1 tablespoon) soy sauce
2 cloves garlic, crushed with sea salt	30ml (2 tablespoons) oyster sauce
5ml (1 teaspoon) grated fresh root ginger	30ml (2 tablespoons) dry sherry
	5ml (1 teaspoon) sugar
450g (1lb) mushrooms (freshly gathered if possible), sliced	5ml (1 teaspoon) sesame seeds
	6 spring onions, finely sliced
225g (8oz) beansprouts	5ml (1 teaspoon) sesame oil

- Heat the olive oil in a frying pan or wok. Add the garlic and ginger and fry for 1 minute. Toss in the mushrooms and stir while they absorb the oil, then add the beansprouts and cook for another minute. Stir in the soy sauce, oyster sauce, sherry and sugar and cook for a further 2 minutes.

- Meanwhile, toast or dry-fry the sesame seeds until golden brown.

- Transfer the stir-fry to a warm serving dish and scatter the sesame seeds and spring onions over the top. Finally, drizzle over the sesame oil.

Perfect Mashed Potatoes

Although the flavour of mashed potatoes depends very much on the variety of potatoes you use, there is a technique to producing that creamy light mash that tempts everyone to have a second helping. If you do not have a choice of organic potato varieties, try to select a floury potato for best results.

450g (1lb) potatoes
sea salt and freshly ground black
   pepper
50ml (2fl oz) milk
	25g (1oz) butter or 30ml (2
	   tablespoons) olive oil, plus extra to
	   serve

- Peel the potatoes and cut them into chunks that are all roughly the same size. Put the potatoes in a pan, cover with cold water and add a good pinch of salt. Cover with a lid and bring to the boil, then turn down the heat and simmer until the potatoes yield to the point of a sharp knife.

- Drain the water from the potatoes, leave the potatoes in the pan and put it back on the hob. Add the milk and let it heat through. Mash the potatoes in the pan, then add the butter and lots of seasoning.

- Pile the potatoes into a warm serving dish and add a final knob of butter or a swirl of olive oil before serving.

Provençal Tian

The name 'tian' comes from a large open terracotta dish made in Provence. It is used to bake fresh seasonal vegetables with eggs, cheese and a little rice. This dish is spectacular made with lovely fresh fronds of purple sprouting broccoli.

1 small onion, chopped	15ml (1 tablespoon) chopped fresh
2 cloves garlic, crushed	herbs
45ml (3 tablespoons) olive oil	sea salt and freshly ground black
450g (1lb) purple sprouting broccoli	pepper
or courgettes	3 eggs
450g (1lb) spinach or chard	100g (4oz) strong cheese (eg
50g (2oz) rice, cooked	Cheddar or Gruyère), grated

- Cook the onion and garlic gently in the oil. Steam the broccoli and spinach until tender but still crisp.

- In a food processor, combine the onion, garlic and greens and process roughly. Add the rice, herbs, seasoning and eggs, plus half the cheese.

- Turn into an oiled gratin dish, sprinkle over the rest of the cheese and bake in a pre-heated moderate oven, 180°C, 350°F, Gas Mark 4, for 35 minutes until puffy and golden brown.

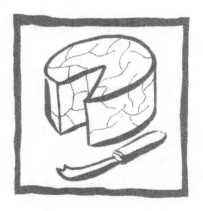

Stuffed Courgette Flowers

When the courgette plants are in full bloom, their lovely yellow flowers brighten up the vegetable patch. It always seems a shame to discard the flowers, especially when they have a delicate and delicious flavour of their own, so here is a recipe to make a really pretty summer dish. Quite often the flowers are attached to small and delicate courgettes and these can be left attached and steamed together with the flowers.

12 courgette flowers
4 sprigs of fresh basil, to garnish

For the tomato sauce
450g (1lb) ripe tomatoes, roughly
    chopped
150ml (¼ pint) water
pinch of cayenne pepper
40g (1½oz) sun-dried tomatoes
sea salt and freshly ground black
    pepper

For the stuffing
1 small onion, finely chopped
1 celery stick, strings removed and
    finely chopped
15g (½oz) butter
25g (1oz) toasted shelled hazelnuts
50g (2oz) pine nuts
100g (4oz) fresh white breadcrumbs
1 egg, beaten
15ml (1 tablespoon) chopped fresh
    basil

- First make the tomato sauce: combine the tomatoes and water in a medium saucepan and bring to the boil. Turn down the heat and cook, covered, until the tomatoes have broken down. Add the cayenne pepper and sun-dried tomatoes and cook for another 5 minutes. Leave the sauce to cool a little before liquidizing. Sieve, then season to taste.

- Make the stuffing: fry the onion and celery in the butter until soft. Mix with the remaining stuffing ingredients, then divide the mixture into 12 equal portions and form into sausage shapes.

- Carefully press a portion of stuffing into each courgette flower, then press the petals around the stuffing. Place the courgette flowers close together in a steamer and steam for 8-10 minutes.

- Gently reheat the tomato sauce and spoon over individual plates. Top each serving with 3 courgette flowers and garnish with a sprig of fresh basil. Serve immediately.

Hot Spinach and Stilton Tatin

This is a colourful dish, full of flavour, ideal to serve at Christmas when there will be Stilton, celery and walnuts in the kitchen. The spinach makes a very good outer cover for the filling, and hides the surprise of the inside. It is quite easy to prepare, and can be made ahead of time and kept warm. Alternatively, it tastes good when cold.

12 large-ish fresh spinach leaves	225g (8oz) carrots, finely grated
1 bunch of spring onions, finely chopped	1 egg
15g (½oz) butter	30ml (2 tablespoons) double cream
50g (2oz) Stilton cheese, crumbled	pinch of freshly ground cumin
50g (2oz) walnuts, chopped	sea salt and freshly ground black pepper
2 celery sticks, strings removed and chopped	

- Blanch the spinach leaves in a pan of boiling water. Drain, then plunge them into cold water to retain their bright green colour. Cut off the stalks and any strong veins in the leaves, then use the leaves to line a 15cm (6in) flan dish. Overlap the leaves and leave enough of them flopping outside the dish to fold back over once the filling is in place.

- Fry the spring onions in the butter until soft but not brown. Mix the Stilton, walnuts, celery and carrots in a bowl, and add the spring onions. Beat the egg, cream, cumin and seasoning together, pour into the bowl containing the other ingredients and mix well.

- Spoon the mixture into the lined flan dish, cover with the overhanging spinach leaves and wrap the whole dish in foil. Place in a roasting tin and pour in enough hot water to come halfway up the side of the dish. Bake in a pre-heated moderate oven, 180°C, 350°F, Gas Mark 4, for 45 minutes.

- To serve, invert the flan dish and turn the flan out upside down. Cut into 4 wedges and serve hot.

Apple Glazed Parsnip Purée

This is a combination made in Heaven! Sweet baked parsnips sharpened with the tang of a good cooking apple. You could serve this dish on its own or as part of a meal when it would accompany a roast, a fish dish, even an omelette. It goes wonderfully well with roast pork or pork sausages.

675g (1½lb) parsnips, peeled or scrubbed and chopped into chunks	1 large cooking apple
sea salt and freshly ground black pepper	juice of ½ lemon
	15ml (1 tablespoon) soft brown sugar

- Steam, boil or microwave the parsnips in a minimum of water. Drain, then mash to a purée and season well. Spread half the purée over the base of a shallow gratin dish.

- Peel, core and very thinly slice the apple. Cover the purée with half the apple slices. Repeat these layers once more, arranging the remaining apple slices neatly on the top and sprinkling over the lemon juice and sugar.

- Bake in a pre-heated moderate oven, 180°C, 350°F, Gas Mark 4, for about 30 minutes or until the apple slices are soft and beginning to brown.

Fish

Can we consider fish that swim in the sea to be organic? Alas, with pollution from ever increasing sources, it has been necessary to produce a standard for organic wild fish. This recently introduced standard will, one hopes, create a new vision for fishing methods and the pollution of our seas. However, at present, the supplies of fish in Britain that meet the standard are limited, Graig Farm (see suppliers, page 174) being at the forefront of development. In the absence of a good supply of registered organic wild fish, I suggest that you select your fish from the best source available to you. A well-established fishmonger who knows where his fish comes from is preferable to a fish stall where the source of the fish is less well catalogued. Buy your fish fresh whenever you can. I do not feel as happy about farmed fish and, wherever possible, will look for the wild alternative. In particular, wild salmon not only has a wonderful flavour but a firmer texture due to the fact that it still swims huge distances each year. Small brown river trout are equally good.

Shellfish are not usually produced through intensive aqua-culture but, again, I would choose shellfish that had come from a natural environment. Even if the shellfish beds have been reseeded by man, at least the fish will have fed and lived in an ever-changing tidal flow. Mussels, cockles and oysters seeded in and around the Menai Straits in North Wales are a classic case. The natural stocks have become depleted over the years and so they have been reseeded by experts who understand that, for the very best growth and flavour, the fish must enjoy tidal feeding in a natural environment.

Fish and Chips

Truthfully, fresh fish in a crisp batter is wonderful. It may not be so good for our health, but done well and eaten not too often, it is a real treat. The first tip is to make sure the fish is fresh, then try to find a potato that fries well. I find that the waxy rather than floury varieties make the best chips.

900g (2lb) waxy potatoes
sunflower or safflower oil, for deep-frying
4 x 175g (6oz) thick pieces of cod, haddock or hake (fillet rather than tail)
salt and freshly ground black pepper
fresh parsley, to garnish

For the beer batter
225g (8oz) self-raising flour
pinch of salt
300ml (½ pint) beer (organic pilsner is the easiest to find)

- First make the batter: tip the flour into a large bowl, add the salt and whisk in the beer a little at a time until you have a smooth batter. Cover and leave to stand for 10 minutes.

- Meanwhile, peel the potatoes and cut them lengthways into chunky chips about 1.25cm (½in) thick. Half fill a deep-fat fryer with oil and heat to 140°C (275°F).

- Blanch the chips in batches in the hot oil for about 5 minutes. They should be cooked through without colouring. Drain them, then tip them into a baking tin lined with kitchen paper.

- Next fry the fish: heat the oil to 160°C (325°F). Season the fish well with salt and pepper and dip the pieces into the batter so that they are completely covered. Deep-fry 2 pieces of fish at a time (don't overcrowd the fryer) for about 8 minutes until the batter is crisp and golden. Drain on kitchen paper and pop into a warm oven.

- Finish off the chips: raise the temperature of the oil to 190°C (375°F) and deep-fry the chips in batches until crisp and golden.

- Serve the fish and chips just as soon as you can, garnished with parsley.

Pan-fried Scallops with Seaweed

This recipe is a particular favourite in Wales, where we are able to source the small scallops or 'queenies' from Cardigan Bay. For those living by the sea in the south, fresh laverbread is available in the markets, but for the rest of us, the canned variety is equally good, or you can use pulped spinach as an alternative. The one golden rule with scallops is not to overcook them or they will become tough.

450g (1lb) scallops (queenies or kings)	1 glass of dry white wine (Welsh if possible)
25g (1oz) butter	salt and freshly ground black pepper
15ml (1 tablespoon) laverbread	15ml (1 tablespoon) double cream or
grated rind of ½ unwaxed orange	fromage frais.

- Clean the scallops and dry them on kitchen paper. Leave the orange corals attached on the little queenies. If using kings, detach the corals and cut each scallop into three.

- In a large frying pan, heat the butter until it sizzles. Toss in half the scallops and fry them quickly so that they cook on all sides. Remove them from the pan as soon as you can and keep them warm in 4 individual serving dishes.

- Add the laverbread to the pan with the orange rind and wine. Boil up well, taste for seasoning and add the cream.

- Pour the sauce over the scallops and serve immediately, with fresh herb rolls or warm herb bread.

Thai Fish in Red Curry

Very much in fashion right now, this Thai fish curry is a way to spice up a fish dish. I have not found a source of organic red curry paste so, when in a hurry, use one of the non-organic ones; but if there is time, it is always fun to make your own using fresh spices.

675g (1½lb) fish fillets (eg cod, haddock, coley)
60ml (4 tablespoons) sunflower or safflower oil
2 onions, finely chopped
1 x 425g (15oz) can tomatoes, drained and chopped

30ml (2 tablespoons) vinegar
10ml (2 teaspoons) red curry paste (see below)
45ml (3 tablespoons) chopped fresh coriander leaves, to garnish

- Skin, bone and cut the fish into 4cm (1½in) chunks.
- Heat the oil and fry the onions gently until soft and golden. Add the tomatoes, vinegar and curry paste and cook the sauce gently for 20 minutes.
- Add the fish, cover and cook until it begins to flake, 5-10 minutes. Taste and adjust seasoning.
- Serve hot, sprinkled with the chopped coriander leaves.

Red Curry Paste
6 dried red chillies
5ml (1 teaspoon) white peppercorns
5ml (1 teaspoon) cumin seeds, dry-fried until brown
5ml (1 teaspoon) coriander seeds, dry-fried until brown
2 shallots, chopped
4 cloves garlic, chopped
15ml (1 tablespoon) chopped fresh root ginger or galangal

15ml (1 tablespoon) chopped fresh lemongrass
15ml (1 tablespoon) grated kaffir or West Indian lime
15ml (1 tablespoon) chopped fresh coriander leaves
15ml (1 tablespoon) kapi (shrimp paste)
salt, to taste
45ml (3 tablespoons) sunflower or safflower oil

- Grind or pound the chillies, peppercorns, cumin and coriander seeds together, then add all the rest of the ingredients.

Makes about 120ml (4½fl oz) or 8 tablespoons.

Salt Baked Sea Bass

This is a great way to cook bass, because the salt crust keeps in all the moisture and so the flavour is terrific. It's equally good for other round fish such as mullet or bream. When you break into the bass and lift out the flesh it has a good aroma of sea salt which brings out the very best flavour of the bass.

1.5kg (3lb) coarse sea salt 2 egg whites	1 whole bass, weighing 1.5kg (3lb), or 2 x 675g (1½lb) whole bass, gutted but not scaled

- Mix the salt with the egg whites and spoon a layer into the bottom of a roasting tin. Place the fish on top, then press the remaining mixture onto the fish, making a thick coat. Make sure that the skin is completely covered and sealed with the salt crust, although covering the tail is not so important. Bake in a pre-heated moderately hot oven, 200°C, 400°F, Gas Mark 6, allowing 30 minutes for the large fish, 20 minutes for the smaller ones.

- To serve, crack the salt crust and lift the fish out, leaving all the salt in the roasting tin. Take the skin off the fish and serve in moist chunks accompanied by a good mayonnaise (see page 88), salsa verde (see page 98) or just a wedge of lemon.

Red Mullet with Samphire and Red Pepper Sauce

Marsh samphire grows here and there around the coast of Great Britain, particularly in East Anglia and the west coast of Wales. It is at its best in early summer and gathering samphire at low tide is one of life's pleasures. Good fishmongers stock samphire regularly, or you can find it pickled, but the flavour and texture is quite different.

225g (8oz) marsh samphire	2 sprigs of fresh thyme
4 x 75-100g (3-4oz) fillets of red mullet	2 cloves garlic, crushed
	5ml (1 teaspoon) coriander seeds
15ml (1 tablespoon) olive oil	2 medium tomatoes, deseeded and chopped
For the red pepper sauce	50ml (2fl oz) white wine
60ml (4 tablespoons) olive oil	salt and freshly ground black pepper
1 shallot, finely chopped	
2 red peppers, deseeded and chopped	

- First make the sauce: heat 15ml (1 tablespoon) of the oil in a pan and sauté the shallot, peppers, thyme, garlic and coriander seeds very gently for 30 minutes. Add the tomatoes and wine and cook for another 10 minutes, then leave to cool.

- Purée the sauce in a food processor or liquidizer, adding the remaining olive oil at the same time. Sieve the sauce, season to taste, and keep warm.

- Wash the samphire thoroughly, then pull off the fleshy leaves and discard the woody stalks. Bring a pan of unsalted water to the boil, add the samphire and boil for 2 minutes. Drain, set aside and keep warm.

- Brush the mullet fillets with the olive oil and season well. Grill for about 4 minutes, 2 minutes on each side.

- Serve the fillets on a mound of samphire, with some red pepper sauce.

Whole Poached Salmon with Fresh Herb Mayonnaise

Nothing is quite so spectacular as serving a whole salmon for a party. Although it can be quite daunting to cook such a large fish for the first time, it really is quite easy. Do take care though, not to overcook it, because whether you poach or bake salmon, it will continue cooking for a good 5-10 minutes when you remove it from the heat.

---

1 whole salmon or sea trout,
weighing 1.8-2.7kg (4-6lb)
salt

3 good handfuls of chopped fresh
herbs (ideally sorrel, dill, chives,
marjoram, basil and parsley)

For the mayonnaise
2 egg yolks or 1 whole egg
300ml (½ pint) best-quality olive oil
15ml (1 tablespoon) white wine or
cider vinegar

For the garnish
thin cucumber slices
lemon slices
bouquets of watercress

- Poach the salmon in gently simmering salted water for 4-6 minutes to the 450g (1lb). Draw the pan off the hob and leave for 30 minutes before removing the fish from the water.

- Skin the fish carefully, remove the head and tail and keep to one side. Carefully lift all 4 fillets off the bone and wrap each individually in foil until needed.

- Make the mayonnaise: whisk the 2 egg yolks together in a small bowl. Continue whisking and add the oil very, very slowly until you have a thick emulsion. Add the vinegar to thin the mayonnaise to the right consistency, then add a pinch of salt and the herbs. Alternatively, you can make mayonnaise in a liquidizer: put the vinegar, whole egg and salt into the machine. With the motor running, gradually add the oil through the hole in the top until you have a thick emulsion.

- To serve, re-assemble the 2 underneath fillets of salmon on a large oval serving dish, then spread with a layer of mayonnaise. Arrange the upper fillets on top and return the head and tail. Garnish with thinly sliced cucumber around the head and down the length of the fish. Add lemon slices and bouquets of watercress and serve the remaining mayonnaise separately.

Trout Wrapped in Bacon

This is a recipe well known to the Welsh, and no doubt it is found in all parts of rural Britain. The combination of well-salted, home-cured bacon and fresh river trout is a good one, and it can be adapted to suit other fish. For example, you can wrap bacon round scallops, oysters or monkfish.

4 good-sized trout	**For the sauce**
15ml (1 tablespoon) chopped chives	Greek yogurt
4 slices of lemon	a little grated fresh horseradish
salt and freshly ground black pepper	a little chopped fresh parsley
8 rashers of smoked streaky bacon	

- Clean, gut and bone the trout. The best way to bone trout is to spread it belly down on a board and press hard along its back – this will loosen the back bone from the flesh. Turn the fish over and, starting at the head end, ease away the back bone with the tip of a knife, removing as many of the small bones as possible at the same time.

- Put some chopped chives and a slice of lemon in the belly of each fish and season with salt and pepper. Wrap each fish in 2 rashers of bacon and arrange them side by side in a baking dish. Bake in a pre-heated moderately hot oven, 200°C, 400°F, Gas Mark 6, for 15-20 minutes until the bacon is crisp on top and the eyes of the fish are white. Meanwhile, mix together the ingredients for the sauce.

- Serve the fish hot, accompanied by the sauce.

Dressed Crab with Lemon Mayonnaise

During the summer months around the coast of Britain, it is quite easy to pick up fresh crab. If you are very lucky, you might come across a fisherman who catches, prepares and delivers his crabs daily to a number of restaurants and local fish shops. This is perfection, otherwise head for your local fish shop and ask for the freshest crabs they can muster. Cock crabs have much more meat in them than hens.

5ml (1 teaspoon) salt
4 live cock crabs, each weighing
    about 675g (1½lb)
lemon mayonnaise (see below), to
    serve

For the garnish
paprika
4 sprigs of fresh parsley
4 wedges of lemon

- Bring a very large pan of water to the boil. Add the salt, then the crabs. Put the lid on the pan to bring the water back to boiling, then simmer for 5 minutes. Turn off the heat and leave the crabs in the pot for another 10 minutes before removing and cooling quickly under the cold tap.

- Working with 1 crab at a time, pull off the legs and prise the body from the under shell with the point of a knife. Remove the inedible 'dead men's fingers' – the feathery looking gills at each side of the body, about a dozen in all. Using as thin an instrument as you can find (ideally a crab pick, but a crochet hook or knitting needle will work well), pick out all the white crab meat. Take out the stomach sac and discard. Scrape out the brown meat around the inside of the shell. Either pick out the legs and claws yourself, or crack them and let the diners do it themselves.

- Wash the crab shells and pile the meat back in, with the brown meat at the sides and the white down the middle. Garnish each dressed crab with a dusting of paprika, a sprig of parsley and a wedge of lemon. Serve with lemon mayonnaise handed separately.

Lemon Mayonnaise
Use the same recipe as that given in Whole Poached Salmon with Fresh Herb Mayonnaise (see page 88), using the grated rind and juice of 1 small unwaxed lemon instead of the vinegar and herbs.

Monkfish and Prawn Kebabs with Lime Dill Butter

This is a great recipe for the barbecue, just take care not to overcook the monkfish. Any firm white fish can be used, such as cod, hake or haddock. If you have a problem finding organic limes, you may prefer to use lemons.

5 unwaxed limes
1 small fresh green chilli, deseeded
    and finely chopped
45ml (3 tablespoons) best-quality
    olive oil
salt and freshly ground black pepper
500g (1¼lb) monkfish
16 uncooked prawns in their shells

For the lime dill butter
2 egg yolks
grated rind and juice of 1 unwaxed
    lime
100g (4oz) butter, diced
30ml (2 tablespoons) chopped fresh
    dill

● Grate the rind and squeeze the juice from 2 of the limes into a dish. Add the chopped chilli and 30ml (2 tablespoons) of the olive oil and season with salt and pepper.

● Skin, bone and cut the monkfish into 2.5cm (1in) cubes. Put the cubes in the dish with the prawns, toss in the marinade, then cover and refrigerate for 1 hour.

● Cut each of the remaining limes into 8 wedges and arrange the wedges alternately on 8 skewers with the fish and prawns. Brush the kebabs with the remaining olive oil and cook over hot coals for 6-7 minutes, turning once and brushing with the marinade.

● Meanwhile, make the lime dill butter: put the egg yolks in a bowl and whisk in the lime rind and juice. Place over a pan of simmering water and gradually whisk in the butter. Continue to whisk until the sauce thickens, then remove from the pan and add the dill.

● Serve the sauce warm, with the kebabs.

Seafood in Saffron Sauce with Garlic Potatoes

This is a family favourite, a simple fish pie that aspires to great heights: luxury fish in a creamy saffron sauce with a garlic potato topping.

a good pinch of saffron threads
175g (6oz) naturally smoked (not dyed) haddock
175g (6oz) cod, haddock or hake
175g (6oz) salmon (preferably wild)
600ml (1 pint) milk
1 bay leaf
½ onion, peeled
50g (2oz) butter
50g (2oz) plain flour
1 glass of dry white wine
50g (2oz) smoked salmon trimmings
100g (4oz) peeled cooked prawns

a good handful of fresh parsley, chopped
50g (2oz) cooked prawns in their shells, to garnish

For the mashed potato topping
900g (2lb) floury potatoes, peeled and cut into equal-sized chunks
salt and freshly ground black pepper
2 cloves garlic, crushed
30ml (2 tablespoons) best-quality olive oil
30ml (2 tablespoons) double cream

- Put the saffron in a teacup and pour over 15ml (1 tablespoon) boiling water. Leave to infuse for 10 minutes.

- Put the smoked haddock, cod and salmon in a pan. Cover with the milk and add the bay leaf, onion and strained saffron water. Bring to the boil and simmer gently for 10 minutes, then leave the fish to cool in the milk. Strain off the milk and reserve. Flake the fish into large chunks, free of skin and bone.

- Make the mashed potato topping: put the potatoes in a pan and cover with cold water. Add salt and the crushed garlic and bring to the boil. Simmer for 20 minutes until soft, then drain the potatoes and return them to the warm pan. Add the olive oil and cream with lots of salt and pepper and mash the potatoes. Set aside.

- Melt the butter in a pan, stir in the flour and cook for 1 minute before adding the strained milk from the fish. Bring the sauce to the boil, add the white wine and season to taste. Add the chunks of flaked fish, the smoked salmon, peeled cooked prawns and the chopped parsley.

- Spoon the fish into a baking dish and cover with the garlic mashed potatoes.

- Fork up the surface and bake in a pre-heated moderately hot oven, 190°C, 375°F, Gas Mark 5, for 20 minutes to heat through and crisp the top.

- Serve hot, garnished with prawns in their shells.

Fiery Cod and Mussel Casserole

This is one of my favourite warming dishes for winter. After a bowl of this fiery cod and mussel casserole, you'll feel full of inner glow, and it is hard to tell whether it's the heat of the dish or the heat of the ingredients. As a recipe it is quick and easy to make, and full of brilliant colour to serve.

1 large onion, sliced
2 cloves garlic, crushed
300ml (½ pint) fish or vegetable stock
45ml (3 tablespoons) balsamic
 vinegar
1-2 dried red chillies, crushed
7.5ml (½ tablespoon) finely chopped
 fresh rosemary
45ml (3 tablespoons) finely chopped
 fresh parsley
2 x 425g (15oz) cans tomatoes,
 chopped

salt and freshly ground black pepper
450g (1lb) firm white fish (eg cod,
 haddock, monkfish, hake), cut into
 2.5cm (1in) cubes
16-20 scrubbed mussels

To serve
4 slices of toasted French bread,
 rubbed with halved cloves garlic
chopped fresh parsley

- Combine the onion, garlic, stock, vinegar and chillies in a large pan. Cover and bring to the boil. Boil for 5-7 minutes. Uncover, lower the heat and simmer until the onion is tender and the liquid almost gone. Stir in the herbs and cook for 1 minute, then add the tomatoes and simmer for 15 minutes. Check the seasoning.

- Add the white fish, cover with a lid and cook gently for 5 minutes. Add the mussels and cook for 2 minutes or until they open. Season to taste.

- To serve, place a slice of toast in 4 shallow soup dishes, ladle the fish and sauce over the toast and sprinkle with a good sprinkling of parsley.

Baked Oysters with Seaweed

At the beginning of the century, oysters were sold for as little as a penny a dozen around the British coast. Today most of the oyster beds are barren due to over fishing, and a new stock of Pacific oysters is being farmed in their place. Happily, big juicy oysters are available all year round now, but alas the price has risen.

50g (2oz) laverbread or soaked and chopped nori, kombu, arame or wakami	50g (2oz) Cheddar cheese, grated
	pinch of freshly grated nutmeg
	freshly ground black pepper
12 oysters, out of their shells	50g (2oz) fresh brown breadcrumbs
150ml (¼ pint) double cream	

- Spread the seaweed over the bottom of 4 shallow flameproof dishes. Arrange the oysters on top, allowing 3 oysters to each dish. Mix the cream with the cheese, nutmeg and pepper and pour over the oysters. Sprinkle over the breadcrumbs.

- Pop under a moderate grill for 10 minutes until bubbling and golden brown on top.

Fillet of Hake with Ginger and Spring Onions

Ideal for those on a diet, this light dish has lots of flavour and all the fun of opening an individual parcel. Serve with soba or udon noodles, tossed in soy sauce and a little brown sugar.

4 x 175g-200g (6-7oz) fillets of hake
30ml (2 tablespoons) sunflower or
  safflower oil
2.5cm (1in) knob of fresh root ginger,
  peeled and finely grated
4 spring onions, chopped

grated rind and juice of 1 unwaxed
  lemon
30ml (2 tablespoons) dry white wine
15ml (1 tablespoon) light soy sauce
salt and freshly ground black pepper

- Remove any bones and skin from the hake. Cut 4 x 30cm (12in) square sheets of baking parchment, greaseproof paper or foil. Brush oil lightly over one side of each square. Place 1 fish fillet in the centre of each square and sprinkle over the ginger, spring onions, lemon rind and juice. Share the wine and soy sauce between them. Season to taste with salt and pepper and drizzle over a little oil.

- Fold the paper to make parcels, leaving lots of room for the steam to circulate but making sure that the juices can't escape during cooking.

- Bake in a pre-heated moderately hot oven, 190°C, 375°F, Gas Mark 5, for 15-20 minutes.

- To serve, place the parcels on individual plates so that your guests can open them themselves. The hake will be moist, the juices full of flavour and the aroma will burst out of the parcel when opened.

Salmon, Shrimp and Lemongrass Fish Cakes

Fish cakes are enjoyed by young and old, and this recipe makes particularly light fish cakes because it combines breadcrumbs with the fish rather than heavier mashed potatoes.

450g (1lb) salmon (preferably wild), cooked and flaked
225g (8oz) peeled cooked shrimps or prawns
2 eggs, beaten
150g (5oz) fresh breadcrumbs
2 fresh lemongrass stems, finely chopped

15ml (1 tablespoon) French mustard
5ml (1 teaspoon) Worcestershire sauce
5ml (1 teaspoon) Cajun spices
30ml (2 tablespoons) chopped fresh parsley
sunflower or safflower oil, for shallow-frying

- Mix all the ingredients together thoroughly. Divide into small patties and place on trays. Cover with greaseproof paper and refrigerate overnight.

- The next day, shallow-fry the fish cakes in hot oil until golden brown on both sides, about 5-6 minutes total cooking time.

- Serve hot, with lemon wedges and homemade mayonnaise or vinaigrette.

Seared Tuna with Coriander and Rice Noodles

To sear tuna you need maximum heat and minimum cooking time. This will ensure that the outside of the fish is blasted with heat and cooked through, leaving the middle very moist. Ideally, a ribbed cast-iron pan is best for this dish. Not only will it cook the tuna well but it will also give those attractive charcoal lines across the surface of the fish. If you do not have one, use a heavy frying pan, or grill the tuna.

4 x 175-200g (6-7oz) tuna steaks
15ml (1 tablespoon) sunflower or
   safflower oil
90ml (3½fl oz) teriyaki sauce (see
   below)
a good bunch of fresh coriander
   leaves, roughly chopped

For the noodles
225g (8oz) rice noodles
15ml (1 tablespoon) sesame oil
1 clove garlic, crushed
2.5cm (1in) knob of fresh root ginger,
   finely grated
1 fresh green chilli, deseeded and
   finely chopped
4 spring onions, sliced

- First cook the noodles: pour boiling water over them and leave them to soak for 3 minutes. Drain and return to the warm pan with the sesame oil, garlic, ginger, chilli and spring onions. Heat this mixture through gently.

- Heat a griddle pan until very hot. Brush the tuna steaks with the oil and griddle for 2-3 minutes on each side. Pour the teriyaki sauce over the tuna and let it bubble up and coat both sides of the fish.

- Serve the tuna steaks with the rice noodles and a very good scattering of fresh coriander leaves over the top.

Teriyaki Sauce
You can buy this in bottles, or make your own by mixing together 50ml (2fl oz) dark soy sauce and 50ml (2fl oz) sake or dry sherry with 25ml (1fl oz) mirin or 5ml (1 teaspoon) sugar.

Skate with Salsa Verde

Fresh skate is a treat to eat – lovely soft flesh with a good flavour. It has no bones, just thick cartilage from which the flesh comes away easily. The tips of the wings are very delicate and you may prefer to trim them before cooking so they don't break up in the pan.

45ml (3 tablespoons) olive oil
4 pieces of skate wing, each about
    175-200g (6-7oz)
freshly ground black pepper
fresh parsley, to garnish

For the salsa verde
2 cloves garlic, crushed
10ml (2 teaspoons) Dijon mustard

45ml (3 tablespoons) chopped fresh
    flat-leaf parsley
15ml (1 tablespoon) chopped fresh
    mint
juice of ½ lemon
30-45ml (2-3 tablespoons) best-
    quality olive oil
sea salt

- First make the salsa verde: combine the garlic, mustard, parsley, mint and lemon juice in a food processor. With the machine running, slowly add the oil until you have a thick, pesto-like sauce. Add salt to taste.

- Heat the olive oil in a large frying pan. Sprinkle the skate with salt, then fry 2 pieces at a time for about 5 minutes on each side, depending on their thickness. Transfer to a warm plate and keep hot while you cook the rest.

- To serve, arrange the skate wings on four warmed plates and spoon the salsa verde to one side. Garnish with fresh parsley.

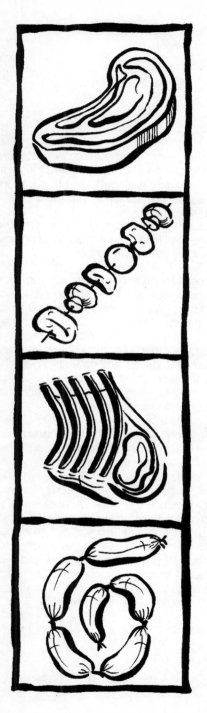

- Soups
- Starters & Snacks
- Salads
- Vegetarian
- Fish
- Meat
- Poultry & Game
- Baking
- Desserts

Meat

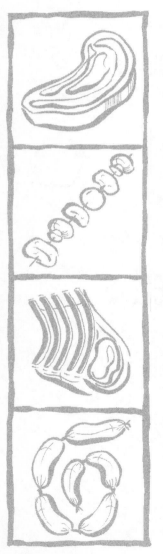

If there was ever a time when consumers needed to know the origin of the meat they eat, it is now. After so many food scares, it is more than just a wise precaution to eat meat from a known source. Even then it is hard to know exactly what ingredients have gone into the feed for the livestock; the actual contents are still rarely disclosed to the farmers.

Organic meat has the benefit of coming from animals whose diet, whether natural herbage or dried feed, is guaranteed to the farmers. Organic farmers take great care with their stock, from the manner in which it is reared – free range rather than intensively – to its welfare when it comes to drugs, and naturally about the food it eats. The greatest care is taken to produce not only hardy stock but breeds that have flavour and fine texture.

Economic forces encourage us as consumers to buy the best quality product at a price we can afford. I suggest that when it comes to organic meat, we must consider whether intensive farming and unnatural animal husbandry produce the meat we really want to eat. If not, then the decision is ours to either follow the force of our convictions and buy organic meat, or opt for leaving meat out of our diet. For me, cheap meat is no option, and I will buy the best I can find. I do not eat as much meat as I used to, but today I look for naturally produced, well-flavoured ingredients.

Spring Lamb with Asparagus

New season Welsh lamb has a delicious but delicate flavour and I think that this recipe, which combines spring lamb with another delicate flavour, that of fresh asparagus, brings out the very best in both ingredients and makes a perfect spring meal. Asparagus sprue (young thin stems) will do rather than the more expensive spears.

900g (2lb) asparagus
15ml (1 tablespoon) olive oil
25g (1oz) butter
900g (2lb) spring lamb, trimmed and
    diced into 2.5cm (1in) cubes
25g (1oz) seasoned flour

4 small onions or shallots, roughly
    chopped
150ml (¼ pint) double cream or
    fromage frais
sea salt and freshly ground black
    pepper
lemon juice, to taste

- Cook the asparagus in 300ml (½ pint) water until tender. (I find the microwave is ideal for cooking asparagus.) Strain off the juice and reserve. Cool the asparagus quickly under the cold tap. Cut off the tips and keep to one side, then liquidize or blend the stems and sieve to make a purée.

- Heat the oil and butter in a large, heavy-based casserole.

- Toss the lamb in the seasoned flour, then fry briskly with the chopped onions. Gradually stir in the liquid in which the asparagus was cooked, then simmer the lamb for about 50 minutes until tender. During cooking, skim off any fat from the surface of the liquid.

- Stir in the asparagus purée and cream, season and add lemon juice to sharpen.

- Serve hot, garnished with the reserved asparagus tips, and with new potatoes tossed in butter with snipped wild garlic and sea salt.

Pork Chops with Juniper and Pears

This is a good casserole dish for the autumn when pears are falling off the trees and organic pork is good. Juniper is one of the best flavours to cook with pork as it adds a fruity sharpness to the meat, and the whole dish benefits from the flavours of the pears, cider and honey. As with all spices, do buy fresh juniper from time to time so that it has its full pungency. You could use loin chops if you prefer.

4-6 sparerib pork chops	300ml (½ pint) dry cider
seasoned flour	2 large pears, peeled, cored and
30ml (2 tablespoons) sunflower or	sliced
safflower oil	10ml (2 teaspoons) honey
1 large onion, chopped	1 bay leaf
5ml (1 teaspoon) juniper berries	1 sprig of fresh thyme
5ml (1 teaspoon) whole black	1 large clove garlic, crushed
peppercorns	5ml (1 teaspoon) sea salt

- Dust the chops with seasoned flour. Heat the oil in a flameproof casserole and brown the chops on both sides in the oil. Remove and fry the chopped onion until soft and golden.

- Meanwhile, crush the juniper berries and peppercorns in a pestle and mortar.

- Return the chops to the casserole with the onions and pour in the cider. Add the pears, honey, crushed berries and peppercorns, bay leaf, thyme, garlic and salt.

- Bring to simmering point, then cover the casserole and cook in a pre-heated very slow oven, 150°C, 300°F, Gas Mark 2, for about 45 minutes.

Sirloin of Beef with Horseradish Cream & Yorkshire Puddings

This is a traditional roast with all the trimmings, but what a difference when you cook the best of organic beef which has been grown on natural herbage, matured slowly and then well hung.

1.5-2kg (3-4 lb) sirloin of beef (either on the bone or boned and rolled)

For the Yorkshire puddings
300ml (½ pint) milk
100g (4oz) plain flour
1 egg
salt and freshly ground black pepper
oil, for brushing

For the horseradish cream
60ml (4 tablespoons) fromage frais or double cream, softly whipped
5ml (1 teaspoon) grated fresh horseradish
a pinch of English mustard powder

- Pre-heat the oven to very hot, 230°C, 450°F, Gas Mark 8, and roast the beef at this temperature for 15 minutes to seal. Reduce the heat to moderately hot, 200°C, 400°F, Gas Mark 6, and cook the beef for 15 minutes per 450g (1lb), allowing an extra 15 minutes. A joint weighing 1.5kg (3lb) will therefore take 1 hour.

- Meanwhile, make the pudding batter with the milk, flour, egg and seasoning. Either put all the ingredients in a liquidizer and blend together, or start with the flour in a bowl and gradually add the other ingredients. Leave the batter to stand for about 30 minutes.

- Once the beef is cooked, allow it to rest in a warm place for about 20 minutes for the juices to settle. This makes the meat firmer to carve.

- Meanwhile, increase the oven temperature to hot, 220°C, 425°F, Gas Mark 7, and heat a bun tin. Brush each little hollow with oil, pour in the Yorkshire pudding batter and bake on a high shelf until risen and golden brown.

- Mix all the ingredients for the horseradish cream together, and add seasoning to taste.

- Dish up the meat and surround with the Yorkshire puddings. Serve the horseradish cream separately.

Honeyed Roast Lamb with Garlic and Ginger

Naturally reared lamb has a splendid flavour and is available just about all the year round now. I find that the honey and spices in this recipe fill the kitchen with wonderful aromas, and everyone is more than ready to sit down and eat once the lamb is cooked.

1.5kg (3lb) leg of lamb
2 cloves garlic, sliced
2.5cm (1in) piece of fresh root ginger, finely grated
grated rind and juice of 1 unwaxed orange

15ml (1 tablespoon) finely chopped fresh thyme
25g (1oz) butter
15ml (1 tablespoon) honey
120ml (4½fl oz) cider
sea salt and freshly ground black pepper

● Using a sharp knife, cut slits in the lamb and insert slivers of garlic into them. Spread the ginger, orange rind and thyme over the outside of the meat. Put the leg of lamb in a roasting tin. Melt the butter with the honey and spread this over the lamb, then pour in half the cider.

● Cover the lamb loosely with foil and roast in a moderately hot oven, 200°C, 400°F, Gas Mark 6, for 20 minutes per 450g (1lb). Halfway through roasting, remove the foil and baste the lamb with the juices.

● When cooked, remove the lamb from the oven and leave to rest for 10 minutes. Meanwhile, drain the fat off the roasting tin and add the rest of the cider to the tin. Boil the juices to reduce to a pouring sauce and add the orange juice. Season to taste.

Japanese Beef with Soba Noodles

This is a delicate way to treat beef and, for those who do not enjoy the fatty aftertaste of eating meat, this is the perfect solution. The soba noodles, which are made from buckwheat, have a lovely nutty flavour and, being wheat free, suit almost all diets. In true Japanese style use only the freshest of ingredients.

225g (8oz) broccoli, trimmed and divided into florets
15ml (1 tablespoon) sunflower or safflower oil
5ml (1 teaspoon) grated fresh root ginger
100g (4oz) small button mushrooms
225g (8oz) sirloin beef, cut into very thin slices and then into 2.5cm (1in) strips
225g (8oz) soba noodles
sea salt

For the simmering stock
15ml (1 tablespoon) sesame oil
15ml (1 tablespoon) sake or dry sherry
15ml (1 tablespoon) rice vinegar or cider vinegar
15ml (1 tablespoon) water
10ml (2 teaspoons) sugar

- First mix together the ingredients for the simmering stock. Set aside.

- Parboil the broccoli until just tender. Drain and set aside.

- Heat the oil in a large frying pan. Add the grated ginger and mushrooms and toss quickly for 1 minute. Add the beef and stir-fry for 2-3 minutes so that it begins to colour. Pour in the stock mixture and bring to the boil, then reduce the heat and simmer, covered, for about 5 minutes or until the beef is cooked through and tender.

- Meanwhile, bring a pan of water to the boil and gently add the noodles, stirring to prevent sticking. Reduce the heat when the pan starts to foam, and simmer according to packet instructions until the noodles are swollen and *al dente*. Drain the noodles and rinse under the cold tap.

- Just before serving, add the broccoli to the beef and heat through. Season.

- Arrange the noodles in individual bowls with the beef and vegetables and spoon over some of the hot stock.

Skewered Lamb with Cardamom

A mixture of lean lamb with lots of Middle Eastern spices. Pride is taken in Arab countries to produce very smooth meat mixtures for this dish, so you may prefer to blend or process the ingredients to make a smooth pâté. These skewers of lamb smell and taste quite wonderful. Serve them with a cooling mixture of yogurt and cucumber, flavoured with fresh mint.

450g (1lb) lean lamb, minced
1 small onion, grated
5ml (1 teaspoon) grated fresh root
  ginger
15ml (1 tablespoon) plain flour
2 cloves garlic, crushed
10ml (2 teaspoons) fresh lemon juice
seeds of 3 cardamom pods, freshly
  ground in a spice mill
2.5ml (½ teaspoon) ground mixed
  spice

good pinch of cayenne pepper
2.5ml (½ teaspoon) coriander seeds,
  freshly ground in a spice mill
15ml (1 tablespoon) natural yogurt
5ml (1 teaspoon) salt

For the yogurt dip
150ml (¼ pint) natural yogurt
½ cucumber, grated
15ml (1 tablespoon) chopped fresh
  mint

● Mix all the ingredients together and leave for 2 hours for the flavours to develop. Meanwhile, soak wooden kebab skewers in cold water.

● Take handfuls of the mixture and press around the skewers. Alternatively, shape into burgers. Grill for 8-10 minutes, turning from time to time.

● Mix together the ingredients for the yogurt dip and serve with the lamb.

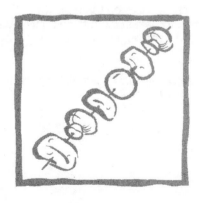

Lamb Shanks with Flageolet Beans

This is a great casserole dish, economical and tasty. Use lamb with lots of flavour, during the late autumn, even mutton if you can find it. Do allow enough time to soak the beans, and then cook the casserole well ahead of time so that the long, slow cooking gives the various ingredients enough time to mellow together.

4 small shanks of lamb, each weighing about 225g (8oz)
2 cloves garlic, sliced
2 tablespoons olive oil
1 onion, finely chopped
375g (12oz) flageolet beans, soaked in cold water overnight

1 x 425g (15oz) can tomatoes, chopped
pinch of sugar
15ml (1 tablespoon) tomato purée
150ml (¼ pint) red wine
sea salt and freshly ground black pepper
1 bunch of fresh parsley, chopped

- Using a sharp knife, cut slits in the lamb shanks and insert slivers of garlic into them. Heat the olive oil in a large flameproof casserole with a tight-fitting lid. Brown the shanks in the hot oil to seal, then remove and keep on one side.

- Add the onion and any remaining garlic to the casserole and fry for about 5 minutes until soft. Drain the beans, add them to the casserole and stir until they are coated in oil. Add the tomatoes, sugar, tomato purée, wine and seasoning. Bring to the boil.

- Return the shanks to the pan, cover and simmer until tender, 1-2 hours. Check after 1 hour and add water, if necessary.

- Stir in the parsley at the last minute and serve with chunks of fresh bread or Perfect Mashed Potatoes (see page 75).

Pork Sheftalia with Parsley

A Cypriot speciality, these pork sausages have a coarse texture and a superb fresh flavour from the parsley. Sheftalia taste especially good when they are hot off the barbecue and served with a squeeze of fresh lemon inside a warmed pocket of pitta bread.

Ask your butcher in advance for the caul. If he is supplying organic pork straight from the farm, it should be no problem for him to ask for the caul too.

225g (8oz) caul (lining from the pig's stomach)
15ml (1 tablespoon) vinegar
450g (1lb) lean pork, coarsely minced
450g (1lb) lean pork, finely minced
1 large onion, grated

60ml (4 tablespoons) chopped fresh parsley (flat-leaf if possible)
10ml (2 teaspoons) sea salt
freshly ground black pepper
lemon wedges, to garnish

- Soak the caul in cold water with the vinegar for 10 minutes.
- In a large bowl, mix the minced porks, onion, parsley, salt and pepper.
- Cut the caul into rectangles, each measuring about 7.5 x 18cm (3 x 7in).
- Put about 15ml (1 tablespoon) filling on the caul and roll into sausage shapes.
- Barbecue the sheftalia over glowing coals or grill them gently so they cook through to the middle.
- Serve hot, garnished with lemon wedges.

Beef in Beer with Rosemary Crust

This stewed beef with a soft herb crust is a great family dish. The beef should be cooked well ahead of time, if possible the day before, so that the best possible flavour can develop.

675g (1½lb) beef (stewing or shin)
225g (8oz) lamb's kidneys (optional)
seasoned plain flour
30ml (2 tablespoons) sunflower or
 safflower oil
2 medium onions, diced
2 leeks, sliced and washed
2 carrots, scrubbed and sliced
300ml (½ pint) beef stock
300ml (½ pint) beer, brown ale or
 pilsner
5ml (1 teaspoon) finely chopped fresh
 rosemary
15ml (1 tablespoon) tomato purée

For the crust
75g (3oz) butter
225g (8oz) self-raising flour
5ml (1 teaspoon) finely chopped fresh
 rosemary
sea salt and freshly ground black
 pepper
1 egg, beaten
a little milk

- Cut the fat and sinew off the beef and kidneys (if using) and dice into 2.5cm (1in) chunks. Toss the meat in seasoned flour. Heat the oil in a heavy-based, flameproof casserole and fry the meat a little at a time so that it browns on all sides. Remove from the pan and fry the onions, leeks and carrots until they colour.

- Replace the meat and add the stock, beer, rosemary and tomato purée. Cover and cook in a pre-heated very slow oven, 150°C, 300°F, Gas Mark 2, for 2 hours.

- Make the crust: rub the butter into the flour and stir in the rosemary and seasoning. Mix the beaten egg with a little milk and add to the flour to make a soft dough. Roll or pat out the dough on a floured surface, then cut into discs with a small cutter.

- Remove the casserole from the oven and increase the heat to hot, 220°C, 425°F, Gas Mark 7. Place the discs of dough on top of the meat, overlapping them a little. Brush with milk, place in the hot oven and bake for 10-15 minutes until the crust is golden brown.

Spiced Breast of Lamb with Fruit Chutney

Great for Christmas, this spiced lamb is something special for a celebration. Prepare it well in advance so that the flavours can blend and develop. Whether as part of a buffet or served in individual portions as a first course, spiced lamb is a treat. You can buy saltpetre from the butcher. It is a very good preservative and helps the lamb maintain its pink colour. It is not essential for this recipe but, if you do not use it, the lamb will only keep for 3-4 days rather than one week.

---

1 breast of lamb
10ml (2 teaspoons) sea salt
5ml (1 teaspoon) freshly ground black
  pepper
pinch each of ground allspice and
  cloves

For the dry marinade
40g (1½oz) coarse sea salt
7g (¼oz) saltpetre (optional)
15g (½oz) soft brown sugar

- Remove the bones from the breast of lamb and cut away excess fat, then sprinkle with the salt, black pepper, ground allspice and cloves. Roll up the lamb and tie or secure with cocktail sticks, then rub over the dry marinade mixture of rock salt, saltpetre (if using) and soft brown sugar.

- Turn the lamb and leave in the refrigerator for up to 1 week (3-4 days without saltpetre). Re-coat the lamb daily with the marinade mixture, which will have become liquid.

- Rinse the lamb well under the cold tap, then put it in a pan and cover with cold water. Simmer until soft when pierced, at least 1 hour. Leave to cool in the cooking liquid.

- Drain the lamb and keep in the refrigerator for at least 12 hours.

- Thinly slice the rolled lamb and serve cold, with sweet fruity chutney.

Tagine of Lamb with Couscous

A tagine is a glazed pottery dish with a wide base and tall funnelled lid, used for cooking on a brazier in Morocco. I think that Moroccan food is among the most exciting in the world, and the slow cooking of a tagine gives a richness that is hard to beat. I first ate a tagine in Marrakesh and loved the combination of spices, meat and fruit. Dried organic fruit does have the most wonderful flavour.

15ml (1 tablespoon) sunflower or
   safflower oil
900g (2lb) leg or shoulder of lamb,
   trimmed and cut into 2.5cm (1in)
   cubes
2 onions, sliced
2 cloves garlic, crushed
5ml (1 teaspoon) grated fresh root
   ginger
good pinch of saffron strands soaked
   in 1 litre (1¾ pints) boiling water

1 cinnamon stick
12 ripe tomatoes, peeled and
   chopped, or 2 x 425g (15oz) cans
   tomatoes, chopped
5ml (1 teaspoon) honey
225g (8oz) pre-soaked prunes
sea salt and freshly ground black
   pepper
450g (1lb) couscous
fresh coriander leaves, to garnish

- Heat the oil in a large, heavy-based casserole. Fry the lamb until well sealed, then remove. Add the onions and cook gently until they begin to caramelize. Add the garlic and ginger and fry for 1 minute, then pour in the saffron water and add the cinnamon. Return the lamb to the pan and cook gently for 50-60 minutes until tender.

- Leave the casserole to cool completely, then remove the lamb and set aside.

- Boil the liquid down until reduced by two-thirds. Add the tomatoes and simmer until reduced by half, then add the honey and prunes and simmer for another 10 minutes. Season to taste, return the lamb to the sauce and heat through until boiling. Keep hot.

- Soak the couscous in an equal volume of warm water until it is completely absorbed, about 10 minutes, then either steam in a colander over boiling water or microwave until cooked through.

- Serve the lamb on a bed of piping hot couscous, with fresh coriander leaves scattered over the top.

Loin of Pork with Chillies

If you can find a range of chilli peppers, then do experiment, for this sauce is strong enough to cope with any amount of heat. As for your diners – only you can say! Do allow plenty of time for the loin to marinate before cooking.

4 jalapeño peppers	5ml (1 teaspoon) coriander seeds
3 fleshy red peppers	½ cinnamon stick
350ml (12fl oz) fresh orange juice	30ml (2 tablespoons) soy sauce
1 small onion, sliced	5ml (1 teaspoon) salt
peeled cloves of 1 whole head of	1.5kg (3lb) loin of pork
garlic	30ml (2 tablespoons) sunflower or
75ml (3fl oz) cider vinegar	safflower oil
5ml (1 teaspoon) cumin seeds	

- Cut the peppers in half and remove the cores and seeds. Grill all the peppers until their skins begin to blister. Remove most of the skin. Liquidize or blend the peppers with the orange juice, onion, garlic and vinegar.

- Grind the cumin and coriander seeds to a powder with the cinnamon stick. Add the spices to the orange juice mixture with the soy sauce and salt.

- Put the loin of pork in a deep dish with a lid and spoon over the sauce. Leave to marinate for at least 6 hours or overnight.

- Lift the pork out of the sauce and drain. Heat the oil in a large roasting tin and sear the pork on all sides.Transfer to a pre-heated moderate oven, 180°C, 350°F, Gas Mark 4, and roast for 30 minutes per 450g (1lb), basting frequently with the sauce.

- Remove the pork from the tin and keep it warm while you boil down the cooking juices and sauce to make a rich colour and flavour.

- Serve the pork sliced, with the sauce.

Herb Pancakes with Stir-fried Pork

As with all stir-fries, once the preparation is done, the dish comes together very quickly. Because the cooking is so fast, always look out for the freshest organic vegetables for a stir-fry; they should be as crisp as possible. These herb pancakes go down well with everyone and they look good due to the pretty flecks of herbs in the batter.

30ml (2 tablespoons) sunflower or safflower oil
225g (8oz) leanest pork loin or fillet, cut into stir-fry strips
2 carrots, peeled and diced
2 cloves garlic, crushed
1 red pepper, deseeded and sliced
1 leek, sliced and washed
5 mushrooms, sliced
10ml (2 teaspoons) grated fresh root ginger

2.5ml (½ teaspoon) cayenne pepper
6 ripe tomatoes, peeled, seeded and chopped, or 1 x 425g (15oz) can tomatoes, chopped
egg white, to seal

For the herb pancakes
100g (4oz) plain flour
300ml (½ pint) milk
1 egg
a good handful of fresh herbs

- First make the pancake batter: liquidize all of the ingredients and leave for 30 minutes to thicken.

- Dry-fry 12 pancakes, cooking the first sides well, but not the second. This way the herbs will look a lovely bright green.

- Heat the oil in a large frying pan or wok. Stir-fry the strips of pork, remove them from the pan and add the carrots. Stir-fry for 1 minute, then add the garlic, red pepper, leek and mushrooms. Stir-fry until soft, then add the ginger, cayenne and tomatoes. Lower the heat and cook for 1 minute. Return the pork to the pan and cook for another minute to heat the meat through.

- Put a spoonful of the mixture in the middle of each pancake, fold into parcels and brush the edges with egg white to seal.

- Just before serving, pop the pancakes into a pre-heated moderately hot oven, 200°C, 400°F, Gas Mark 6, to crisp up for a few minutes.

Pork with Red Wine and Coriander

This combination of tender pork cooked with crushed coriander seeds and red wine is one of the most successful dishes from Cyprus, where it is usually served with a nutty cracked wheat pilaff (page 67) and a bowl of thick Greek yogurt.

675g (1½lb) lean pork, cut into 2.5cm (1in) cubes
15-30ml (1-2 tablespoons) light olive oil
fresh coriander leaves, to garnish

For the marinade
200ml (7fl oz) red wine
15ml (1 tablespoon) coriander seeds, finely crushed
1 cinnamon stick
sea salt and freshly ground black pepper

- First mix together all the ingredients for the marinade. Pour the marinade over the cubed pork and leave to marinate in the refrigerator for at least 4 hours, or overnight if possible.

- Drain the pork and reserve the marinade. Heat the oil in a heavy-based, flameproof casserole and brown the cubes of pork a few at a time until they are all crisp and brown. Drain off any excess oil from the pan, then return all the pork and the marinade to the pan together with seasoning and enough water to just cover the meat. Bring to the boil.

- Cover the casserole, lower the heat and cook gently on the hob or in a pre-heated moderate oven, 160°C, 325°F, Gas Mark 3, for about 30 minutes until the pork is tender. Almost all of the liquid should have evaporated to leave a thick sauce: if necessary, cook the pork uncovered for a further 10 minutes to reduce excess liquid.

- Serve the pork hot, garnished with fresh coriander leaves.

Rack of Lamb with Lavender

The sweet flavour and succulence of organic lamb is maximized by roasting the rack of lamb quickly in a very hot oven. If you prefer, you could use rosemary rather than lavender – the flavour will be excellent, but you will miss out on the tantalizing aroma of the lavender in the crust.

5ml (1 teaspoon) fresh lavender	50g (2oz) brown breadcrumbs
75g (3oz) cream cheese	675-900g (1½-2lb) loin or best end of
1 clove garlic, crushed	neck of lamb, skinned and chined

- Chop the lavender finely or grind it to a powder. Mix it with the cream cheese, garlic and breadcrumbs, then press this mixture together with a palette knife and spread over the fat side of the lamb.

- Put the lamb in a roasting tin and cook in a pre-heated hot oven, 220°C, 425°F, Gas Mark 7, for 30 minutes, or a little longer if you don't like your lamb pink.

- Serve the lamb cut down between the rib bones, either as single cutlets or doubles.

- Serve with a moist vegetable dish and perhaps some redcurrant jelly.

- Soups
- Starters & Snacks
- Salads
- Vegetarian
- Fish
- Meat
- **Poultry & Game**
- Baking
- Desserts

Poultry & Game

Do you remember how good roast chicken used to taste? It is hardly surprising, when I think of how chickens in my youth used to scratch around the farm yard, stretching their legs, picking at this and that and living a great deal longer than they do today. Happily, it is now possible to buy free-range chickens that have been raised on a natural diet with no growth promoters and antibiotics in their feed. However, there is another reason why chicken tastes so bland today. It simply is not hung anymore, and so the flavours do not have time to develop.

Game does still hang, of course, and the flavour of a well-hung pheasant is hard to beat. Pigeon, too, has a superb flavour when hung, as do all the game birds. Modern, farmed venison suffers least from not being hung and still has a good rich flavour. For the most part, farmed venison is well reared, humanely slaughtered and wonderfully tender.

Chicken with Lemon, Honey and Garlic

Known as 'sticky chicken' in our family, I seem to have been making this dish for decades because it always goes down so well with my children and their friends.

The sharpness of the lemon brings out the best flavour of the chicken, while the honey and garlic give this delicious dish a rich aroma. I usually use runny honey, but stiff honey can be softened within half a minute in the microwave.

4 chicken breasts, skinned
2 cloves garlic
sea salt and freshly ground black
   pepper
	30ml (2 tablespoons) honey
	grated rind and juice of 2 unwaxed
	   lemons

- Arrange the chicken breasts in a shallow ovenproof dish. Peel and crush the garlic with a pinch of salt. Warm the honey a little if it is stiff, then mix it with the garlic and the grated lemon rind and juice. Season with salt and pepper.

- Pour this sticky mixture over the chicken and leave to marinate for at least 2 hours, turning from time to time.

- Bake the chicken breasts in a pre-heated moderately hot oven, 190°C, 375°F, Gas Mark 5, for about 45 minutes, turning once so that both sides begin to colour. Test to make sure it is cooked through – no pink juices should run when the chicken is pierced with a sharp knife.

- Serve the chicken in its own juices, with Perfect Mashed Potatoes (see page 75) and a fresh herb green salad.

Breast of Duck with Plums and Balsamic Vinegar

Sometimes in the heat of summer it is hard to find the enthusiasm to put together a smart meal for family or friends. Here is the answer, a quick and simple meal that is stunning to look at and wonderful to eat. Breasts of duck are readily available, and plums are at their best from July through to the beginning of September.

4 duck breasts
15-30ml (1-2 tablespoons) balsamic
  vinegar
15ml (1 tablespoon) honey
6-8 good-sized plums, halved and
  stoned

2.5ml (½ teaspoon) allspice berries,
  crushed
sea salt and freshly ground black
  pepper

- Heat a large, flameproof casserole and gently cook the duck breasts, skin side down, until the fat melts and the skin crisps and turns golden. Add the vinegar, honey, plums, allspice and seasoning. Cover and cook gently for 15-20 minutes.

- Remove the duck breasts and cut into 5mm (¼in) slices. Arrange them on warmed individual plates or down the centre of a large serving dish.

- Drain off the excess fat from the casserole, bring the remaining juices to the boil and reduce down to a syrupy consistency. Spoon the sauce around the duck.

- Serve with a salad of green leaves and herbs dressed with walnut oil.

Cinnamon Chicken with Almonds

I was given this recipe by Ken Goody, a friend who ran a popular restaurant in Harlech. Although he has now retired, his friends still recall those great days when dishes like this were readily available at his establishment.

It is a party recipe, to serve 6 people.

6 chicken breasts, skinned	2.5ml (½ teaspoon) cayenne pepper
30ml (2 tablespoons) sunflower or	or chilli powder
safflower oil	5cm (2in) piece of fresh root ginger,
12 cardamom pods	peeled
6 cloves	8 cloves garlic, peeled
5cm (2in) cinnamon stick	50g (2oz) flaked almonds
2 medium onions, finely chopped	7.5ml (1½ teaspoons) sea salt
5ml (1 teaspoon) coriander seeds,	150ml (¼ pint) single cream
freshly ground in a spice mill	150ml (¼ pint) natural yogurt
5ml (1 teaspoon) cumin seeds, freshly	15ml (1 tablespoon) sultanas
ground in a spice mill	(optional)
	chopped fresh coriander, to garnish

- Gently brown the chicken breasts on both sides in the hot oil. Remove and set aside. In the same pan, fry the cardamoms, cloves and cinnamon for 1 minute, then add the chopped onions and fry until golden and soft.

- Add the coriander, cumin and cayenne, stir well and fry for 4 minutes.

- In a blender, whizz the ginger, garlic and almonds, adding sufficient water to produce a paste with a consistency like thick cream. Stir this paste into the mixture and cook for 3-4 minutes.

- Add the chicken, cream and yogurt, stir well and add a little water to cover if necessary, then add the sultanas if using. Cover and simmer for 30 minutes, or place in a pre-heated moderate oven, 180°C, 350°F, Gas Mark 4, for 45 minutes.

- Sprinkle with chopped coriander and serve with rice, chutney, slices of banana and a salad.

Venison with Coriander Seeds and Leek and Potato Rösti

Farmed venison is lean and tender and is usually much younger than wild venison, so it has a milder, gamey flavour. I treat it rather like steak, taking care not to overcook it since it is important to retain all the juices and so keep it moist. For this recipe, the venison steaks are set on top of individual potato röstis to make a smart party dish, but served with a bowlful of mashed potatoes, the venison tastes just as well.

5ml (1 teaspoon) coriander seeds, crushed
1 glass of red wine
4 x 175g (6oz) venison loin steaks
15ml (1 tablespoon) sunflower or safflower oil
juice of ½ orange,
5ml (1 teaspoon) redcurrant jelly

For the rösti
2 large potatoes
1 medium leek
sea salt and freshly ground black pepper
15ml (1 tablespoon) sunflower or safflower oil

- Add the crushed coriander seeds to the wine and pour over the venison. Leave to marinate for at least 1 hour.

- Make the rösti: peel and grate the potatoes and leek and mix with seasoning. (Do not soak the potatoes in water because you need their starch to keep the rösti together.) Heat the oil in a large pan and fry 4 mounds of the rösti gently, turning once to brown both sides. Take out of the pan and keep warm.

- Heat the remaining oil and fry the venison steaks briskly to seal on both sides. Lower the heat and cook for 4 minutes until tender and pink in the middle.

- Place a rösti on each of 4 warmed plates, slice the venison steaks and arrange them on top. Add the marinade to the pan juices and stir well, then add the orange juice and redcurrant jelly. Boil to reduce by half, taste for seasoning and pour around the steaks.

Chargrilled Chicken Fajitas

A great family favourite, this Mexican dish of pancakes or tortillas wrapped around a peppery chicken filling with avocado and soured cream dips is messy to eat and great fun! Alas, I have not located any organic tortillas, but homemade ones work well, and the flavour of free-range organic chicken will make this a very special dish.

30ml (2 tablespoons) olive oil
2 cloves garlic, crushed
30ml (2 tablespoons) lime juice
15ml (1 tablespoon) chopped fresh
  parsley
1 sprig of fresh thyme, chopped
pinch of cayenne pepper
sea salt and freshly ground black
  pepper
4 chicken breasts, skinned
1 jalapeño pepper or 1 small green
  chilli, deseeded and chopped
1 red pepper, deseeded and cut into
  strips
1 large onion, sliced
soured cream, to serve

For the flour tortillas
175g (6oz) unbleached flour
5ml (1 teaspoon) baking powder
2.5ml (½ teaspoon) salt
60ml (4 tablespoons) white vegetable
  shortening
120ml (4½fl oz) warm water

For the avocado dip
1 large ripe avocado
5ml (1 teaspoon) Worcestershire
  sauce
5ml (1 teaspoon) fresh lemon juice

- First make the tortillas: in a bowl, mix the dry ingredients together. Rub in the fat until it is evenly mixed and add the water to make a stiff dough. Turn onto a floured board and knead for 5 minutes. Alternatively, use a food processor. Leave the dough to rest for 30 minutes.

- Divide the dough into 8 pieces and roll out to make 25cm (10in) tortillas. Griddle or dry-fry as you would pancakes. Wrap in a damp tea towel until ready to use.

- Make the filling: make a marinade with 15ml (1 tablespoon) of the oil, half the garlic, the lime juice, herbs, cayenne and seasoning. Pour over the chicken breasts and leave for at least 1 hour.

- Heat a large frying pan and heat the remaining oil in it, then fry the remaining garlic and the jalapeño gently so they do not brown. Add the red pepper and onion and cook until they just begin to turn translucent. They should still be slightly crisp.

- Chargrill or griddle the chicken breasts, turning once and basting with the marinade. Meanwhile, make the avocado dip: peel the avocado, cut it in half lengthways and remove the stone. Mash the flesh and mix with the Worcestershire sauce and lemon juice.

- To serve, slice the chicken into thin strips. Warm the tortillas through and then wrap them around some of the chicken and pepper filling, folding them into a manageable shape to eat. Serve the avocado dip and some soured cream separately.

Salt Duck with Onion Sauce

This recipe comes from a collection of recipes first published in 1867 by a very remarkable woman called Lady Llanover. English by origin, when Augusta Hall married and lived near Abergavenny in Wales, she was determined to improve the standard of living of all who lived around her, so she closed all the pubs! Shortly after, she set to writing her cookery book, *The First Principles of Good Cookery*.

The recipe is very simple and particularly good, but do remember to allow 3 days for the dish to be ready.

100g (4oz) sea salt	50ml (2fl oz) water
1.75-2.25kg (4-5lb) duck	15ml (1 tablespoon) plain flour
	300ml (½ pint) milk
For the sauce	sea salt and freshly ground black
2 medium onions, chopped	pepper

- Rub the salt well into the skin of the duck. Leave in the refrigerator for 3 days, turning and re-coating the duck with the resulting liquid every day.

- Thoroughly rinse the salt off the duck and put the bird into a large pan or casserole. Pour over cold water to cover, bring to the boil and simmer very gently for 1½ hours, turning the bird over halfway through.

- Make the sauce: stew the chopped onions in the water very, very gently for about 15 minutes until tender. (It may be necessary to press some greaseproof paper down on top of the onions to retain the moisture.) Strain off what liquid is left, adding 15ml (1 tablespoon) water if necessary, and whisk it with the flour. Whisk in the milk, then add this mixture to the onions. Bring the sauce to the boil and simmer for 1-2 minutes to cook the flour and thicken the sauce, then either liquidize or sieve. Taste for seasoning.

- Serve the duck sliced, with the sauce.

Rabbit with Mustard and Thyme

Wild rabbit is much more available now, particularly through good fish and game shops. It has a lovely flavour and can make a most satisfying meal, especially when cooked with herbs and mustard.

15ml (1 tablespoon) sunflower or safflower oil	300-400ml (10-14fl oz) chicken or vegetable stock
25g (1oz) butter	1 good sprig of fresh thyme
675g (1½lb) jointed rabbit	sea salt and freshly ground black pepper
4 good leeks, sliced and washed	
2 cloves garlic, crushed	150ml (¼ pint) thick cream or fromage frais
15-30ml (1-2 tablespoons) plain flour	
30ml (2 tablespoons) wholegrain mustard	fresh lemon juice, to taste

- In a large, heavy-based casserole, heat the oil and butter and fry the rabbit until golden on all sides. Remove the rabbit and toss in the leeks and garlic. Stir until beginning to soften, then add enough flour to absorb the oil. Stir in the mustard, pour over the stock and replace the rabbit. Add the thyme and seasoning.

- Cover the pan and cook very gently for 1½ hours until the rabbit is tender, stirring occasionally.

- Add the cream and stir until well blended. Taste for seasoning and add some fresh lemon juice to sharpen if necessary.

Thai Green Chicken Curry

Thai cooking is so popular at the moment that I have included this recipe, although I am not aware that organic coconut milk or prepared green curry paste is available at the moment. Just remember, to buy a chicken with the best possible flavour, make it organic!

1 x 425g (15oz) can coconut milk
15-30ml (1-2 tablespoons) green
  curry paste
1.6kg (3½ lb) chicken, jointed, or 6
  chicken breasts, skinned
30ml (2 tablespoons) fish sauce

2 sprigs of tender citrus leaves or
  kaffir lime leaves, or 2 fresh
  lemongrass stems
30ml (2 tablespoons) finely chopped
  deseeded fresh green chillies
60ml (4 tablespoons) finely chopped
  fresh basil or coriander leaves

• Reserve one-third of the coconut milk and pour the rest into a heavy-based casserole. Bring to the boil and simmer until reduced by half. Add the curry paste and cook this sauce until the oil begins to separate out.

• Add the pieces of chicken and cook over low heat for 10 minutes, turning them from time to time until sealed. Add the remaining coconut milk mixed with a cup of water, then add the fish sauce and citrus leaves. Bring to the boil.

• Reduce the heat and simmer, uncovered, for 35-40 minutes for chicken joints, 20-25 minutes for breasts. The chicken should be well cooked and tender and the gravy rich and oily.

• Stir in the chopped fresh chillies and herbs, simmer for 5 minutes longer, then turn into a warmed serving dish. Serve with aromatic Basmati rice.

Pheasant Casserole with White Wine and Juniper Berries

The hardest part of preparing a casserole is gathering all the ingredients. Once they are safely in the pot, then you can sit back and wait until the casserole is ready, savouring the aromas as it cooks.

a brace of oven-ready pheasants, each bird weighing about 675g (1½lb)
45ml (3 tablespoons) olive oil
½ bottle of dry white wine
60ml (4 tablespoons) white wine vinegar
grated rind of 1 unwaxed orange
2 sprigs of fresh sage
2 sprigs of fresh rosemary
2 cloves garlic, crushed
5 cloves

15ml (1 tablespoon) juniper berries, crushed
sea salt and freshly ground black pepper
fresh parsley, to garnish

For the pheasant stock
a few carrot peelings
1 onion
1 small bunch of fresh herbs
1 celery stick

- First joint the pheasants: with a pair of sharp kitchen scissors, remove the legs and cut the wings away. Finally, leaving the breast meat attached to the bone, cut the whole breast away from the remaining carcass. Divide the breast in half lengthways.

- Make a pheasant stock: put the carcasses in a large saucepan and cover with cold water. Add the carrot peelings, onion, fresh herbs and celery. Simmer gently for about 1 hour, then strain and boil hard until reduced to about 600ml (1 pint).

- Heat the oil in a large, heavy-based casserole and brown the pheasant joints. Add the stock and the rest of the ingredients and simmer the pheasant very, very gently for 1 hour or until tender.

- Take the pheasant joints out of the casserole and trim the pieces, cutting away any superfluous bone. Pile the joints in a warmed serving dish and keep hot. Boil up the sauce and reduce by half until you have a syrupy consistency, then strain and pour over the pheasant.

- Serve hot, garnished with parsley.

Warm Salad of Pigeon Breast with Pine nuts

For a quick salad, I simply cut the breasts away from the whole carcass of the pigeon. The lean and tender pigeon breasts have a rich gamey flavour, just right for a warm salad.

a selection of salad leaves	15ml (1 tablespoon) olive oil
4 rashers of streaky bacon, snipped into dice	2 pigeon breasts, cut into slivers
100g (4oz) field mushrooms, sliced	10ml (2 teaspoons) cider vinegar
50g (2oz) pine nuts	15ml (1 tablespoon) walnut oil
	chopped fresh parsley, to garnish

- Arrange the clean, dry salad leaves on 4 individual plates.

- In a large, heavy frying pan, gently dry-fry the bacon until the fat runs. Add the mushrooms and allow them to absorb the bacon fat, then add the pine nuts and turn up the heat, stirring all the time. Add the olive oil and toss in the slivers of pigeon breast. Stir over brisk heat to seal the meat on all sides, then cook through for a further 1-2 minutes.

- Scatter the pigeon, bacon, mushrooms and pine nuts over the salad leaves.

- Deglaze the pan with the cider vinegar, heating gently and stirring to collect the juices. Take the pan off the heat, add the walnut oil and blend well, then pour over the salads.

- Garnish with chopped parsley and serve at once, with nut and herb rolls.

Roast Pheasant with Port and Orange Gravy

There is no shortage of pheasants these days, but consider the diet of the birds and try to source your pheasant from a shoot over moorland rather than in an area of cultivation. The former have a better flavour because birds that forage for their food are more active, develop more muscle, which is what we eat, and so often have a more pronounced flavour. Birds that are fed regularly often potter about waiting for the next feed, and they do literally taste more fatty.

Here is a recipe that really makes the most of a brace of pheasants, a dish fit for a celebration, even Christmas if you wanted to ring the changes from turkey.

75g (3oz) butter, softened
grated rind of 2 unwaxed oranges
5-10ml (1-2 teaspoons) chopped
  fresh thyme
sea salt and freshly ground black
  pepper
a brace of oven-ready pheasants,
  each bird weighing about 675g
  (1½lb)
1 orange, cut into 8 segments
8 rashers of streaky bacon
watercress, to garnish

For the stuffing balls
5 spring onions, chopped
50g (2oz) butter

6 slices of mixed wholegrain bread,
  crumbed
15ml (1 tablespoon) chopped fresh
  mixed herbs
5ml (1 teaspoon) finely grated
  unwaxed orange rind
beaten egg, to bind

For the bacon rolls
6 rashers of streaky bacon
12 no-need-to-soak dried prunes or
  apricots (or a mixture of both)

For the gravy
juice of 2 unwaxed oranges
150ml (¼ pint) port
15ml (1 tablespoon) redcurrant jelly

- Beat together the butter, orange rind, thyme and seasoning. Squeeze about a tablespoon of this butter under the breast skin of both birds and spread the remainder over the surface. Pop 1 orange segment inside each cavity and then lay 4 rashers of bacon over each bird.

- Roast in a pre-heated moderately hot oven, 200°C, 400°F, Gas Mark 6, for 30 minutes. Add the remaining orange segments to the roasting tin and roast, basting regularly, for a further 30-60 minutes, depending on the size of birds.

- Meanwhile, make the stuffing balls: cook the onions gently in the butter until soft. Add the breadcrumbs, herbs and orange rind and just enough beaten egg to bind the mixture together. Shape into 12 balls.

- Make the bacon rolls: de-rind the bacon and cut each rasher in half crossways. Wrap a piece of bacon around a prune or an apricot.

- Cook the stuffing balls and bacon rolls in the oven for the last 15 minutes of the pheasants' cooking time. To test if the pheasants are done, pierce the thighs and the juices should run clear.

- Dish up the birds and keep warm with the stuffing and bacon rolls. Spoon off the excess fat from the roasting tin and let the juices bubble up well on the hob. Add the orange juice and port, stirring well to reduce a little, then add the redcurrant jelly. Season to taste.

- Serve the gravy with the roast pheasants and trimmings.

Chicken with Spinach and Tamari

Chicken breasts have become the food of the nineties – quick and easy to prepare, enjoyed by most people and yet, all too often, bland. If there is an advantage to cooking chicken breasts, first choose organic chicken and then add some extra flavour yourself!

The spinach, garlic and Japanese soy sauce tamari gives the chicken an oriental lift.

30ml (2 tablespoons) olive oil
4 chicken breasts, skinned and
  boned
8 spring onions, chopped, or 2 small
  leeks, sliced and washed
2 cloves garlic, crushed
5ml (1 teaspoon) finely grated fresh
  root ginger

450g (1lb) spinach, well washed
15ml (1 tablespoon) tamari or light
  soy sauce
sea salt and freshly ground black
  pepper
toasted sesame seeds, to garnish

- Heat the oil in a large, heavy-based casserole and fry the chicken breasts for 2 -3 minutes on each side until they begin to colour. Take out of the pan and set aside. Add the spring onions, garlic and ginger and fry for 2 minutes, then stir in the spinach, tossing to coat as much of it as possible in the oil.

- When the spinach begins to wilt, stir in the tamari and seasoning, then return the chicken to the pan. Cover with a lid and simmer gently for 15-20 minutes until the chicken is cooked.

- Take out the chicken and cut each breast into about 5 slices. Arrange the spinach on 4 warmed plates and place the chicken slices on top. Boil the juices left in the pan quickly to reduce to a syrupy consistency, spoon over the chicken and garnish with toasted sesame seeds.

Roast Quails with Bacon

Although I have not come across organically reared quails, I do have a supply that I know and trust where the birds are reared in a natural environment and without additive-laden feed.

Buy quail ready boned if you can, they are so much easier to eat. This recipe gives a stuffing that will add flavour and the bacon coating helps to keep the flesh moist.

100g (4oz) basmati rice
sea salt and freshly ground black
  pepper
8 quails
30ml (2 tablespoons) olive oil
1 medium onion, chopped
1 clove garlic, crushed
75g (3oz) pine nuts, toasted

75g (3oz) no-need-to-soak dried
  apricots, chopped
grated rind and juice of ½ unwaxed
  orange
15ml (1 tablespoon) chopped fresh
  parsley
5ml (1 teaspoon) coriander seeds,
  crushed
8 good rashers of smoked streaky
  bacon, de-rinded

- Cook the rice in a pan of salted water and leave to drain.

- Wash the quails inside and out under gently running cold water. Pat dry with kitchen paper.

- Heat the oil in a large pan and cook the onion and garlic gently until soft. Add the rice, pine nuts, apricots, orange rind and juice, parsley, coriander and seasoning. Spoon some of this mixture into the cavity of each quail, leaving a little space for expansion because the filling cooks inside the birds.

- Stretch each bacon rasher with the back of a knife blade to make it longer, then cut each crossways in half. Wrap 2 pieces of bacon around each quail so that the breasts are well covered.

- Arrange the quails in a roasting tin and roast in a pre-heated moderately hot oven, 200°C, 400°F, Gas Mark 6, for 20-25 minutes.

- Serve the quails, 2 to a plate, with the juices poured over. Fruity chutney tastes great with this dish.

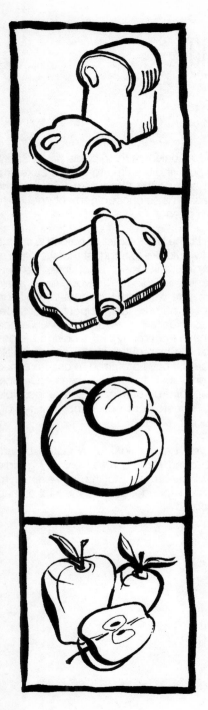

Baking

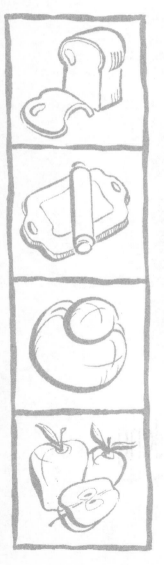

Is good home baking a thing of the past? Sadly, few of us now find the time to bake a cake or a loaf of bread, yet the pleasure it brings to the recipients should be encouragement enough to bake more often.

Returning home to the smell of baking is such a treat that I would like to suggest that we bake at least once a week using, of course, the very best organic ingredients. Flavour wins again here. There are wonderful flavours in the flour, fresh spices, natural fats, superb chocolate, fresh fruits, excellent dried fruit and unrefined sugars. I have tried many of the baking recipes using organic sugar, but since it is only available as granulated, I have preferred to use unrefined raw caster sugar in some cases. (Organic cane syrup or fructose powder are possible alternative sweeteners but, I find, not terribly successful in baking.)

Whether you bake a loaf of wheaten bread, some sun-dried tomato rolls, savoury griddle scones, blackcurrant muffins or even gin-soaked lemon sponge, get into the kitchen and start baking now!

Sun-dried Tomato Rolls

Organic flour is now readily available and you will have the choice of unbleached white, wholemeal, wholewheat, spelt, or a range of alternatives from barley, buckwheat, millet or rye to soya. To give the rolls the right texture, I suggest that at least half of your flour should be unbleached white, with alternative flours making up the rest. Ascorbic acid acts as a natural rising agent and will speed up your baking.

675g (1½lb) strong unbleached white flour	25mg tablet ascorbic acid (available from the chemist as vitamin C)
5ml (1 teaspoon) salt	about 375ml (13fl oz) warm water
25g (1oz) fresh yeast	15ml (1 tablespoon) olive oil
5ml (1 teaspoon) sugar	50g (2oz) sun-dried tomatoes, chopped

- Sift the flour and salt into a large bowl. Cream the fresh yeast with the sugar, ascorbic acid and a few spoonfuls of the warm water. Leave until frothy, then add to the flour and mix in enough warm water to make a firm dough. Add the olive oil and sun-dried tomatoes and knead the dough for at least 5 minutes, or until the dough is soft and pliable, like playdough.

- Shape the dough into 24 rolls the size of tangerines and arrange on an oiled baking sheet. Leave to rise in a warm place for about 30 minutes until doubled in size.

- Bake in a pre-heated very hot oven, 230°C, 450°F, Gas Mark 8, for 20 minutes.

- Serve warm.

Pesto Rolls
Replace the sun-dried tomatoes with 30ml (2 tablespoons) pesto.

Walnut Rolls.
Replace the olive oil with 15ml (1 tablespoon) walnut oil and the sun-dried tomatoes with100g (4oz) chopped walnuts.

Focaccia
Make the dough without the sun-dried tomatoes. Brush a little oil over 2 baking sheets and divide the dough into two. Flatten the pieces of dough and spread them out on the baking sheets. Leave to rise in a warm place for 1 hour until puffy. Poke holes in the dough with your finger and drizzle olive oil into them all. Scatter over either coarse sea salt, chopped fresh rosemary, olives, shallot or onion, or a combination of some or all of these things. Bake as for the rolls.

Irish Soda Bread

One of the best memories I have of the year I spent in Ulster was eating warm soda bread, straight out of the oven. It is so easy to make I don't understand why I don't make it more often. Speed is important for the dough starts to rise as soon as the dry ingredients come into contact with the milk.

Buttermilk, an important ingredient, is not always easy to find, but I use fresh milk and a good squeeze of lemon juice or yogurt instead.

450g (1lb) unbleached plain white
   flour
5ml (1 teaspoon) salt
2.5ml (½ teaspoon) bicarbonate of
   soda

2.5ml (½ teaspoon) cream of tartar
300ml (½ pint) buttermilk, sour milk or
   natural yogurt, to mix

- In a bowl, mix the flour and salt together. Sift in the bicarbonate of soda and cream of tartar to make sure there are no lumps. Using a metal spoon, mix lightly and quickly with the buttermilk, sour milk or yogurt, adding just sufficient to give a soft, but not sticky, dough. It is difficult to give an exact quantity of liquid because this varies with the flour.

- Immediately turn the dough onto a lightly floured board and shape it into a round cake using floured hands. Mark out 4 farls, or quarter the dough and transfer to a baking sheet.

- Bake in a pre-heated hot oven, 220°C, 425°F, Gas Mark 7, for about 30 minutes, according to the thickness.

- Wrap in a clean cloth to cool if you want to keep the soda bread soft.

Wheaten Bread

This is a recipe for a coarse, nutty wheaten loaf, which my family just loves. We find that wheaten bread should be eaten fresh, so this recipe does not make too large a loaf – in fact it can easily be eaten at one sitting.

If you cannot find buttermilk, add a good squeeze of fresh lemon juice to fresh milk or use half water and half milk.

225g (8oz) wholewheat flour	5ml (1 teaspoon) bicarbonate of soda
100g (4oz) unbleached plain white flour	5ml (1 teaspoon) cream of tartar
5ml (1 teaspoon) salt	25g (1oz) butter
25g (1oz) unrefined soft brown sugar	300ml (½ pint) buttermilk

- In a large bowl, mix the flours together with the salt and sugar.

- Sift in the bicarbonate of soda and cream of tartar to make sure there are no lumps.

- Rub in the butter, then pour in the buttermilk and work quickly to make a dough.

- Turn the dough out onto a floured board and shape into a round loaf. Mark out 4 farls and dust the top with a little extra wholewheat flour.

- Bake at once in a pre-heated moderately hot oven, 200°C, 400°F, Gas Mark 6, for about 40 minutes until risen and crisp on top.

Celtic Oatcakes

Although traditional Celtic oatcakes are made purely from oatmeal and water, I must admit to cheating a little because the original mixture tastes quite dull and is extremely brittle to prepare. My recipe includes some wholewheat flour as well as oatmeal and a little extra butter for flavour. These oatcakes can be cooked on a griddle but I find it easier to lay them on a baking tray and bake them in the oven.

175g (6oz) medium or fine oatmeal
175g (6oz) wholewheat flour
5ml (1 teaspoon) salt
1.25ml (¼ teaspoon) bicarbonate of
   soda

75g (3oz) butter or margarine
about 30ml (2 tablespoons) cold
   water

- In a large bowl, mix the oatmeal, flour, salt and bicarbonate of soda. Rub in the butter with your fingers until the mixture looks like breadcrumbs. Mix to a soft, but not sticky, dough with cold water.

- Turn the dough out onto a board dusted with wholewheat flour and roll out to a thickness of about 3mm (⅛in). Cut the dough into discs with a pastry cutter and arrange on a baking sheet.

- Bake in a pre-heated moderate oven,160°C, 325°F, Gas Mark 3, for about 20 minutes until pale golden.

Carrot Cake with Lemon Crème Fraîche

This cake is at its best made with organic carrots. Their extra flavour makes all the difference and the sweetness is superb. Serve with a dollop of tangy lemon crème fraîche for a really special treat.

175g (6oz) butter
225g (8oz) unrefined caster sugar
2 eggs, beaten
225g (8oz) self-raising flour
5ml (1 teaspoon) ground cinnamon or mixed spice
pinch of salt
225g (8oz) carrots, scraped or peeled and grated
100g (4oz) walnuts, chopped (optional)

For the lemon crème fraîche
150ml (¼ pint) crème fraîche
grated rind and juice of ½ unwaxed lemon
unrefined caster sugar, to taste

- Grease and line a 1.2 litre (2 pint) loaf tin.Cream the butter with the sugar until very soft. Beat in the eggs, a little at a time. Fold the flour, spice and salt into the creamed mixture with a large metal spoon. Stir in the carrots and nuts (if using) and turn the mixture at once into the prepared tin.

- Bake in a pre-heated moderate oven, 180°C, 350°F, Gas Mark 4, for 1¼ hours until cooked right through and crisp and golden on top. Cool on a rack.

- For the lemon crème fraîche, simply mix the ingredients together, adding sugar to suit your taste.

Cheese and Bacon Griddle Scones

When my children were small, these savoury griddle scones were one of their favourite teatime treats. Quick to make and full of goodness, rather than sweetness, I was always pleased to make up a batch before bath time.

100g (4oz) self-raising flour	30ml (2 tablespoons) chopped bacon
1 large egg	or ham
150ml (¼ pint) milk	30ml (2 tablespoons) grated cheese

- Put the flour into a small bowl, add the egg and pour in the milk a little at a time, whisking until you have a thick batter.

- Whisk or beat with a fork until the batter is smooth, then add the bacon and cheese.

- Grease and heat a heavy frying pan or griddle. Drop tablespoonfuls of the batter onto the hot pan and cook until bubbles appear. Turn the scones over and cook the other sides for 1 minute until cooked through.

- Serve just as they are, spread with butter, or with a drizzle of maple syrup.

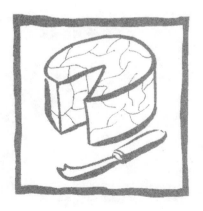

Walnut and Banana Bread

Ripe bananas are so sweet and full of flavour that they need no extra sugar to encourage them to give a great flavour to this bread. So here is a healthy and satisfying teatime treat that will keep most of the sweet-toothed brigade happy too.

3 very ripe, soft bananas	2.5ml (½ teaspoon) ground nutmeg
175g (6oz) soft vegetable margarine	175g (6oz) wholewheat flour
grated rind of 1 unwaxed orange	3 eggs
5ml (1 teaspoon) bicarbonate of soda	100g (4oz) walnut pieces
2.5ml (½ teaspoon) ground cinnamon	

- Purée the bananas in a food processor or liquidizer. Add the margarine and orange rind to the purée and beat or process until smooth. Stir the bicarbonate of soda and spices into the flour and add to the mixture alternately with the eggs.

- Fold in the walnut pieces and spoon the mixture into a well-greased 1.2 litre (2 pint) loaf tin or a 20cm (8in) diameter cake tin. Bake in a pre-heated moderately hot oven, 190°C, 375°F, Gas Mark 5, for 30 minutes or until firm.

- Cool the cake in the tin for 5 minutes, then turn out onto a rack to cool completely.

Bara Brith

'Bara brith', translated from Welsh, means speckled bread, a loaf dotted with mixed fruit and spice. At one time it would have been made from the last of the dough after a day's baking, more often now it is prepared as a cake without yeast.

450g (1lb) mixed raisins, sultanas and currants	90ml (6 tablespoons) unrefined soft brown sugar
300ml (½ pint) cold tea	5ml (1 teaspoon) ground mixed spice
30ml (2 tablespoons) marmalade	450g (1lb) self-raising flour
1 egg, beaten	runny honey, to glaze

- Soak the fruit in the tea overnight.

- The next day, mix in the marmalade, egg, sugar, spice and flour. Spoon into a greased 1.2 litre (2 pint) loaf tin. Bake in a pre-heated moderate oven, 160°C, 325°F, Gas Mark 3, for 1¾ hours or until the centre is cooked through. Check from time to time to see that the top does not brown too much, and cover with a sheet of foil if necessary.

- Leave the bara brith to stand in the tin for 5 minutes, then turn it out onto a rack.

- While the cake is warm, brush honey over the top to glaze.

Gin-soaked Lemon Sponge

A firm favourite, this delicious sponge dripping with lemon syrup makes a great teatime treat, and with the addition of a little gin, it becomes something very special.

225g (8oz) soft margarine	**For the topping**
225g (8oz) unrefined caster sugar	juice of 1 lemon
275g (10oz) self-raising flour	a good tot of gin
5ml (1 teaspoon) baking powder	30ml (2 tablespoons) unrefined
4 eggs	granulated sugar
grated rind of 1 unwaxed lemon	
about 10ml (2 teaspoons) milk	

- Put all the sponge ingredients in a bowl and beat until smooth. Adjust to a soft dropping consistency with the milk.

- Spoon the mixture into a greased and lined 1.5kg (3lb) cake tin or 2 x 1.2 litre (2 pint) loaf tins. Bake in a pre-heated moderately hot oven, 190°C, 375°F, Gas Mark 5, for 45-50 minutes until lightly browned.

- Mix the ingredients for the topping and pour over the cake while it is still hot.

- Leave the cake to cool in the tin for 30 minutes before removing.

Apple Cake

This is a recipe from a good friend, Elunid Lloyd, who runs a hotel in Pembrokeshire. Elunid believes that the best flavour comes from wild or natural ingredients and will often scour the local countryside for herbs and greens. This cake seldom lasts long once made!

100g (4oz) butter or vegetable margarine	225g (8oz) wholemeal self-raising flour
100g (4oz) unrefined soft brown sugar	5ml (1 teaspoon) ground mixed spice
2 eggs	4 tart eating apples
grated rind and juice of 1 unwaxed lemon	honey, to serve

- Butter a 20cm (8in) square cake tin or a 450g (1lb) loaf tin.

- Cream together the butter and sugar, beating hard, and always for longer than you anticipate. Add the eggs with the lemon rind and juice. Fold in the flour and spice, which will give a fairly stiff consistency, and put the mixture in the tin.

- Peel, core and slice the apples, then arrange the slices all over the top of the sponge mixture so that they stick up rather like bristles on a hedgehog. Flick a little water over the top.

- Bake in a pre-heated moderately hot oven, 190°C, 375°F, Gas Mark 5, for 40-50 minutes or until a sharp knife inserted into the centre of the cake comes out clean.

- Drizzle honey over the top of the warm loaf and serve warm or cold.

Welsh Cakes

These little cakes are cooked on a bakestone and although all the Celtic countries use the bakestone it is only the Welsh who griddle these sweet cakes. A heavy frying pan works well, but take care not to let the sugar in your Welsh Cakes cause them to burn.

225g (8oz) self-raising flour	75g (3oz) currants
pinch of salt	2.5ml (½ teaspoon) ground mixed
100g (4oz) butter or vegetable	spice
margarine	5ml (1 teaspoon) honey
75g (3oz) unrefined caster sugar, plus	1 medium egg, beaten
extra for dusting	

- Sift the flour and salt into a bowl, then rub in the fat until the mixture resembles breadcrumbs. Stir in the sugar, currants, mixed spice and honey. Mix to a firm dough with the beaten egg.

- On a floured board, roll or pat out the mixture until 1.25cm (½in) thick. Cut into 6.25cm (2½in) discs and griddle over medium heat until golden on both sides.

- Dust the Welsh cakes with sugar and eat immediately, or store in an airtight tin.

Blackcurrant Muffins

Muffins are the most adaptable of buns, and I find that this recipe works well with almost any fruit. If you do not have any blackcurrants, you could use raspberries or blackberries, even strawberries if they are diced. Recently I have made banana muffins with a hint of cinnamon. These muffins keep well in an airtight tin for a couple of days but few last that long in my kitchen.

150g (5oz) unbleached plain white flour
75g (3oz) unrefined caster sugar
15ml (1 tablespoon) baking powder
1 egg
75ml (3fl oz) milk
75g (3oz) soft vegetable margarine
75g (3oz) blackcurrants, topped and tailed

For the topping
25g (1oz) unrefined caster sugar
5ml (1 teaspoon) ground mixed spice

- Grease and flour 15 deep bun tins. In a food processor, mix the flour, sugar and baking powder. Combine the egg with the milk and add to the dry ingredients with the soft margarine. Process until smooth. (If making the muffins by hand, first beat the margarine with the sugar, then beat in the egg and add the flour and baking powder. Finally, add the milk.)

- Fold in the blackcurrants by hand and spoon the mixture into the prepared bun tins, filling them only three-quarters full. Mix the sugar and spice together and sprinkle over the tops of the buns. Bake in a pre-heated moderate oven, 180°C, 350°F, Gas Mark 4, for 20 minutes.

Double Chocolate Chip Cookies

These cookies are simply delicious when made with organic chocolate. The extra flavour shines through and it is very, very hard to keep away from them once they are out of the oven. If you have ever wondered what the fuss is all about when comparing chocolate made in Britain to that made in Switzerland, the difference is totally apparent when biting into organic chocolate for the first time. Here is a richness that sits on your tongue like silk, a flavour that explodes in your mouth, and an aftertaste that lingers on and on and on.

175g (6oz) unbleached plain white flour	60g (2½oz) unrefined soft brown sugar
2.5ml (½ teaspoon) bicarbonate of soda	2.5ml (½ teaspoon) vanilla essence
pinch of salt	1 egg
60g (2½ oz) butter	75g (3oz) dark chocolate, coarsely grated
75g (3oz) organic or unrefined granulated sugar	75g (3oz) milk or white chocolate, coarsely grated

- Stir together the flour, bicarbonate of soda and salt. Beat the butter, sugars and vanilla essence together. Add the egg and beat well. Gradually add the flour mixture, beating well. Stir in the grated chocolate.

- Drop rounded teaspoonfuls of the mixture onto an ungreased baking sheet. Bake in a pre-heated moderately hot oven, 190°C, 375°F, Gas Mark 5, for about 7-8 minutes or until lightly brown.

- Cool slightly before removing to a rack or they will be too soft to move.

Sticky Gingerbread

Although the Americans have been advocates of maple syrup for decades, we have yet to discover the marvellous rich and natural flavour that it gives to our food. I have used it rather than treacle in this recipe with remarkably successful results and I think that the texture and flavour of this gingerbread is as good as any. Now that I have a bottle of organic maple syrup in my cupboard, it is surprising just how often it finds its way into my recipes!

100g (4oz) unbleached plain white flour	1 egg
2.5ml (½ teaspoon) bicarbonate of soda	100g (4oz) unrefined soft brown sugar
pinch of salt	45ml (3 tablespoons) maple syrup
5ml (1 teaspoon) ground ginger	100ml (4floz) soured cream
5ml (1 teaspoon) ground mixed spice	50g (2oz) white vegetable fat, melted

- Mix the flour with the bicarbonate of soda, salt and spices. Beat the egg with the sugar, maple syrup, soured cream and vegetable fat. Stir in the flour mixture and beat for 1 minute.

- Pour the gingerbread mixture into a 1.2 litre (2 pint) loaf tin or cake tin and bake in a pre-heated moderate oven, 180°C, 350°F, Gas Mark 4, for 30 minutes.

- Leave in an airtight tin for at least 2 days and preferably up to 1 week before serving.

Date Shortcake

I first made this shortbread when I ran a stall in a Saturday market in Fleet, Hants. If custom was slow, and the winter wind was biting, this shortbread was the first to be eaten by the team standing behind the stall! This very simple recipe makes the best of organic dates and brings a chewy texture and good crunch to these shortbread fingers. Ideal for a picnic, or just something to nibble.

175g (6oz) butter or vegetable margarine	175g (6oz) dates, stoned and chopped
225g (8oz) self-raising flour	unrefined caster sugar, to serve
100g (4oz) unrefined soft brown sugar	

- Rub the butter into the flour. Stir in the sugar and dates and mix well.

- Press the mixture into a shallow tin so that it is about 1.25cm (½in) thick. Bake in a pre-heated moderate oven, 180°C, 350°F, Gas Mark 4, for 30-40 minutes.

- Cut into fingers while still warm and dust the top with caster sugar.

Desserts

As a nation, we are definitely growing a sweeter tooth and desserts are eaten more now than ever before. In the past, the pudding was often the cheapest and most filling part of the meal and Mother relied on it to fill up the family after a frugal portion of meat.

Today, we are blessed with an enormous choice of sweet things to eat, but since few of us really need a lot of sugar, perhaps we should decide to choose only the best and enjoy a little rather than a lot.

With the world trade market making seasonal fruits available to us all the year round, we are spoilt for choice. However, the pleasure of gathering and eating fruit as it comes into season locally is still worth savouring.

I have tried to give a selection of desserts to suit all tastes. Sharp fruit compotes, sticky puddings, rich mousses, exotic ice creams, hot family fillers and sophisticated tarts. I hope that there is something for everyone.

Summer Fruits with Oatmeal Cream

Everyone always asks for more of this simple but delicious pudding. The soaked oatmeal has a lovely nutty flavour which blends well with the fruit. During the winter I use frozen summer fruit or make up a fruit salad from fresh and dried fruit.

100g (4oz) medium oatmeal	sugar, to taste
30ml (2 tablespoons) heather honey	225g (8oz) summer fruits
300ml (½ pint) Greek yogurt	

- Soak all but a spoonful of the oatmeal in cold water overnight.

- The next day, strain off any excess water from the soaking oatmeal and stir in the honey, yogurt and enough sugar to suit your taste. Arrange the fruit in the bottom of a large glass bowl or individual wine glasses. Spoon over the oatmeal cream so that it sits on top of the fruit.

- Toast the remaining oatmeal under the grill, or dry-fry in a frying pan, until brown and nutty. Scatter over the pudding.

- Serve chilled.

Lime and Lemon Tart

Sweet, sharp and tangy, this citrus tart cleans the palate. It may be rather fiddly to prepare, but well worth the effort. If you cannot find organic limes and prefer to use oranges, the recipe works well, but the sharpness of the lemon is important. Try to plan ahead and leave a few hours for the fruit to flavour the cream before baking, it makes all the difference to the flavour of the tart.

125g (4½oz) unsalted butter	**For the filling**
75g (3oz) icing sugar	2 eggs
1 egg yolk	125g (4½oz) caster sugar
1 whole egg	grated rind and juice of 1 unwaxed
250g (9oz) plain flour	lime
	grated rind and juice of 1 unwaxed
	lemon
	175ml (6fl oz) double cream

- First make the pastry: cream the butter with the icing sugar until very pale, then add the egg yolk and whole egg and beat hard. Fold in the flour and mix to a firm paste. Chill in the refrigerator for 30 minutes.

- Roll out the pastry and use to line a 20cm (8in) flan tin or dish. Press thick strips of foil around the sides to prevent the pastry collapsing during baking.

- Bake in a pre-heated very hot oven, 230°C, 450°F, Gas Mark 8, for 8-10 minutes , just to set the pastry. Remove from the oven and remove the foil strips. Reduce the oven temperature to moderate, 180°C, 350°F, Gas Mark 4.

- Prepare the filling: cream the eggs with the caster sugar until light in colour, then add the rind and juice of the lime and lemon. If possible, leave to infuse for a couple of hours before baking. Pour the filling through a sieve into a bowl (to remove the rind) and stir in the cream.

- Pour the custard mixture into the pastry case and bake in the oven for 15-20 minutes.

- Serve warm or cold.

Rhubarb Compote and Hazelnut Crumble

An all-time favourite, Sunday lunch just wouldn't be right without a fruit crumble. You can vary the ingredients to suit the seasons. Try plum and almond, gooseberry and elderflower, apple and blackberry, etc. The nuts can also vary. Try almonds or walnuts if you prefer, but personally I think the taste and smell of toasting hazelnuts is hard to beat.

450g (1lb) rhubarb
grated rind and juice of 1 unwaxed orange
5ml (1 teaspoon) grated fresh root ginger
50g (2oz) unrefined caster sugar
100g (4oz) self-raising wholemeal flour

pinch of salt
50g (2oz) butter or vegetable margarine
50g (2oz) demerara sugar
5ml (1 teaspoon) ground mixed spice
50g (2oz) chopped hazelnuts

- Cut the rhubarb into 2.5cm (1in) sticks and put in the bottom of a 1.2 litre (2 pint) pie dish. Add the grated rind and juice of the orange, the ginger and caster sugar.

- In a large bowl, mix the flour and salt. Using your fingertips, rub in the butter until the mixture looks like breadcrumbs. Stir in the demerara sugar, spice and nuts.

- Spoon the crumble mixture over the rhubarb and bake in a pre-heated moderate oven, 180°C, 350°F, Gas Mark 4, for 30 minutes until crisp and golden.

Oranges with Maple Syrup and Cardamom

Oranges are often at their best in the middle of winter, so look out for some of the large juicy ones. I always like to find the blood oranges in the shops just after Christmas. This cardamom spice dish with a hint of maple syrup will bring a warm glow. The range of organic fruit available is expanding all the time – perhaps you will be able to find some sweet navel oranges.

6 large, thin-skinned sweet oranges   6 cardamom pods
30ml (2 tablespoons) maple syrup

- With a sharp serrated knife, peel the oranges over a bowl to collect the juices – use a gentle sawing movement to remove the orange skin in one long strip as you might peel an apple. Remove the segments of the oranges from between the membranes. This is best done by sliding a knife alongside the membrane towards the centre of the orange and then pushing the knife out away from the centre, so cutting the fruit free. Keep all of the juice.

- Heat the orange juice gently and add the maple syrup.

- Remove the seeds from the cardamom pods and crush them coarsely.

- Arrange the oranges in a bowl, pour over the syrup and scatter over the crushed cardamom seeds.

- Serve warm.

Gooseberry Cream with Elderflower

This is a combination of flavours made in heaven. Nature has certainly played a part in this blend of flavours since they both appear in early summer, and often end up in the same dish. Gooseberries are not so easy to come by these days, but they do freeze well, especially when they have been poached. You might consider growing your own gooseberries and there are some particularly delicious varieties available.

As for elderflowers, elder is not always easy to spot at other times, but the clouds of tiny white flowers and the strong musty smell is very evident at the end of May. Look for elder in the hedgerow, it flowers for about three weeks.

450g (1lb) gooseberries	each sugar and water and a head
30ml (2 tablespoons) elderflower	of fresh elderflower
syrup, or 30ml (2 tablespoons)	300ml (½ pint) double cream

- Top and tail the gooseberries and put them in a glass dish or casserole. Add the elderflower syrup, or the sugar, water and elderflower head. Cook gently in the microwave or in a pre-heated moderate oven, 180°C (350°F) Gas Mark 4, until soft. Leave to cool, then push through a sieve. Chill in the refrigerator.

- Whisk the cream so that it is thick but not stiff. Fold the chilled gooseberry purée gently into the cream so that it is not fully amalgamated.

- Serve in a large glass bowl or wine glasses.

Baked Peaches with White Wine

I often find that some of the summer fruits lack their full flavour due to early harvesting. For peaches and apricots a little bit of cooking really improves the taste. Look out for a fragrant white wine; there are a good selection of organic ones available.

100g (4oz) ground almonds	5ml (1 teaspoon) almond essence,
100g (4oz) ricotta or cream cheese	orange flower water or rosewater
15ml (1 tablespoon) unrefined caster sugar	4 good-sized peaches or nectarines, or 8 apricots, greengages or plums
	100ml (4fl oz) white wine

- Mix together the ground almonds, ricotta, sugar and almond essence.
- Cut the fruit in half, remove the stones and fill the cavities with the almond mixture.
- Arrange the fruit in a baking dish, pour round the wine and bake in a pre-heated moderately hot oven, 200°C, 400°F, Gas Mark 6, for 15 minutes.
- Serve the baked peaches hot, with crème fraîche.

Fresh Figs with Yogurt and Macadamia Nuts

When I lived in Cyprus, each season brought it owns excitement with the food grown on the island. During the spring, when the vegetation shot up, Cypriots would gather armfuls of lush greens from the roadside. Then, during the summer, we gorged ourselves on grapes, melons, cherries, strawberries and finally, as the heat began to die away, came my favourite, fresh figs. Served simply, to enjoy their flavour and wonderful colours, this recipe couldn't be easier.

4 large ripe figs, or 8 if they are small	50g (2oz) fresh macadamia nuts,
150ml (¼ pint) Greek yogurt	chopped
15ml (1 tablespoon) runny honey	

- Simply cut each fig from the top downwards like segmenting an orange, but leave the base intact. Open the figs out like flowers, to expose the wonderful colour of the flesh.

- Sit 1 fig on each of 4 serving plates, spoon some yogurt in the centre of each fruit and drizzle the honey around the edge of the plate. Scatter the chopped macadamia nuts on top of the honey.

Apple Galette

Although it may take a little time to prepare, this apple galette makes a wonderful pudding for a crowd. It works well at any time of year, but particularly in the autumn when cooking apples are at their best. Windfalls would be perfect for this recipe.

For the pancakes
300ml (½ pint) milk or milk with a
   drop of light ale added
1 whole egg
1 egg yolk
15ml (1 tablespoon) melted butter
50g (2oz) wholemeal flour
50g (2oz) plain flour

For the filling
900g (2lb) cooking apples
50g (2oz) butter
100g (4oz) unrefined caster sugar
5ml (1 teaspoon) ground mixed spice
50g (2oz) sultanas

For the topping
100g (4oz) unrefined soft brown
   sugar
knobs of butter

- Whizz all the ingredients for the pancakes in a food processor or liquidizer. Leave the batter to stand for 30 minutes to thicken.

- Meanwhile, prepare the filling: peel, core and chop the apples, then fry them gently in the butter until beginning to soften. Add the sugar, spice and sultanas and cook gently to a soft mush. Remove from the heat.

- Make 12 pancakes in the usual way.

- Butter an ovenproof dish and lay a pancake flat on the bottom. Cover with a good tablespoon of the filling, then add another pancake. Now top with more filling and add another pancake. Continue layering and filling the pancakes until all are used up.

- Sprinkle the soft brown sugar over the pancake dome and dot with the butter. Bake in a pre-heated hot oven, 220°C, 425°F, Gas Mark 7, for 15 minutes.

Rice and Nutmeg Brulée

What better way to bury those gloomy thoughts about the onset of autumn than to cook up some comfort food to bring solace to the soul. Rice pudding is definitely the type of dish that makes me feel good, especially with the extra flavour of nutmeg. Full-cream milk is the best to use, semi-skimmed milk tends to make a thin, watery rice pudding.

600ml (1 pint) milk
40g (1½oz) pudding or Carolina rice
45ml (3 tablespoons) unrefined caster
  sugar

2.5ml (½ teaspoon) freshly grated
  nutmeg

- Butter a flameproof baking dish and pour in the milk. Add the rice, 30ml (2 tablespoons) of the sugar and the nutmeg and bake in a pre-heated moderate oven, 160°C, 325°F, Gas Mark 3, for 2 hours.

- Leave the rice to cool, then sprinkle the remaining sugar over the surface. Caramelize the top by popping the dish under a pre-heated hot grill until the sugar melts and the top turns golden.

- Chill before serving.

Cherry Clafoutis

This is a very easy recipe to put together for those of us who enjoy a warm pudding at the end of the meal. It is simply fresh fruit baked in a batter. The recipe is from the Limousin region of France where the soft fruit is wonderful. Cherries are the traditional fruit to use for a clafoutis but you can use plums, damsons, apricots, currants, raspberries or blackberries for this recipe.

450g (1lb) fresh cherries, stoned	**To serve**
3 eggs	30-45ml (2-3 tablespoons) brandy
150g (5oz) plain flour	icing sugar
75g (3oz) soft brown sugar	
150ml (¼ pint) full-fat milk	

- Butter a 25cm (10in) baking dish and arrange the cherries over the base.

- Whisk the eggs, flour, sugar and milk together until well mixed. Pour this batter over the cherries.

- Place the dish on a baking sheet and bake in a pre-heated moderately hot oven, 190°C, 375°F, Gas Mark 5, for 35-40 minutes or until the batter is puffed up and golden brown.

- Remove the clafoutis from the oven and allow to cool. It may sink a little.

- Before serving, spoon over the brandy and dust with icing sugar.

Sticky Toffee Pudding

This recipe is for those people who really appreciate its rich sweet flavour and sticky texture...which is just about everyone I know!

100g (4oz) butter
350g (12oz) unrefined soft brown
  sugar
2 eggs
450g (1lb) plain flour
5ml (1 teaspoon) baking powder
7.5ml (1½ teaspoons) bicarbonate of
  soda
450ml (¾ pint) boiling water

For the sauce
150g (5oz) unrefined soft brown
  sugar
100g (4oz) butter
300ml (½ pint) double cream

- Lightly grease a large baking dish. Cream the butter and sugar together, adding the eggs gradually. Fold in the flour, baking powder and bicarbonate of soda and pour in the boiling water. Beat the batter until smooth, then pour into the baking dish.

- Bake in a pre-heated moderate oven, 180°C, 350°F, Gas Mark 4, for 35-40 minutes.

- Make the sauce: put the sugar, butter and cream in a pan. Bring to the boil, stirring, and simmer for 3 minutes.

- Pour a little of the sauce over the hot pudding and return to the oven for a few minutes.

- Serve the pudding hot from the oven, with the remaining sauce and extra cream or vanilla ice cream.

Chill-out Chocolate Cake

Light, luscious and remarkably delicious, this chocolate cake is nothing more than layers of meringue mixed with the very best chocolate cream. Organic chocolate has revolutionized chocolate puddings because of its depth of flavour.

For the meringues
4 egg whites
225g (8oz) unrefined caster sugar

For the filling
225g (8oz) dark chocolate
100ml (4fl oz) cold coffee
600ml (1 pint) double cream

For the topping
100g (4oz) dark chocolate, grated

- Line 3 baking sheets with non-stick baking parchment.

- Make the meringues: whisk the egg whites until very stiff (so that you can turn the bowl upside down without the meringue falling out). Whisk in half the sugar, making sure that the meringue still keeps its body, then fold in the remaining sugar.

- Spread the meringue on the paper in 3 circles of the same size.

- Bake in a pre-heated very slow oven, 140°C, 275°F, Gas Mark 1, for 1 hour until crisp and dry. It doesn't matter if the meringues turn a little golden or crack.

- Make the filling: break up the chocolate and put it in a heatproof bowl with the coffee. Suspend the bowl over a pan of simmering water, making sure that the bottom of the bowl does not touch the hot water. Stir the mixture until the chocolate melts, then remove the bowl from the pan and leave the mixture to cool.

- Whisk the cream to a thick but not stiff consistency and fold together with the cooled chocolate. (It should make a thick, spreadable cream.)

- Arrange a meringue circle on a large serving plate and spread chocolate cream right over the top. Layer up both the other meringues on top, covering them completely in the chocolate cream. Finally, spread chocolate cream around the sides so that no meringue is visible. Decorate the cake with the grated chocolate – scatter it over the top and press it onto the sides with a palette knife.

- Chill the cake for at least 2 hours before serving.

Mango and Lime Ice Cream

When you come across a fragrantly ripe mango, seize it and make this incredible ice cream. Served after a hot and spicy curry, it is perfect.

Happily there is no need to whisk this ice cream by hand half way through the freezing process, simply pop it into the freezer and forget about it.

1 large ripe mango	grated rind and juice of 2 unwaxed
150ml (¼ pint) double cream	limes
150ml (¼ pint) natural yogurt	unrefined sugar, to taste

- Peel and stone the mango, then mash the flesh until it is a purée.

- Whisk the cream until it is the same consistency as the yogurt. Fold the yogurt and cream together, then stir in the mango purée and lime rind and juice. Add enough sugar to make a sweet cream, remembering that some of the sweetness will be lost when it is frozen.

- Freeze until firm.

Chocolate Pots

This chocolate cream contains raw egg and is very rich. A dollop of whipped cream looks pretty on top, or you can leave the pots quite plain. Although this recipe is even easier to make than a chocolate mousse, I think that it really is better. Compared to a light mousse, the cream in these chocolate pots has the most wonderful silky rich texture that is so satisfying and a concentrated flavour that will be appreciated by everyone, especially chocoholics. There is nothing that can take the place of chocolate!

225g (8oz) plain chocolate	1 egg
300ml (½ pint) single cream	15ml (1 tablespoon) brandy

- Coarsely grate the chocolate over the cream in a saucepan. Heat gently until the chocolate has melted – do not let the cream boil.
- Remove from the heat, add the egg and brandy and whisk until smooth and creamy.
- Pour the chocolate cream into little pots or ramekins and leave to set in the refrigerator for 3 hours or overnight.
- Serve chilled, with plain, crisp biscuits.

Berries in Red Wine with Woodruff

Henry VIII so enjoyed his puddings that it was not unknown for him to reward the inventor of a successful new recipe with an extravagant gift, say a small manor house! One of his favourite recipes was berries soaked or 'seethed' overnight in wine and sweetened with honey and woodruff. Woodruff or sweet woodruff, a hardy perennial, is a lovely plant to grow in a flower border. With clusters of white flowers, it has the scent of new-mown hay and, when dried, the leaves make good scented pillows. Alternatives might be sweet cicely, camomile, bay or even sweet marjoram.

450g (1lb) unblemished berries (eg
   strawberries, raspberries,
   blackberries)
15ml (1 tablespoon) runny honey

1 good sprig of woodruff, or orange
   or lemon mint
300ml (½ pint) full-bodied red wine

● Hull the berries and put them in a deep bowl, taking care not to bruise them. Stir the honey and woodruff into the wine and pour over the berries.

● Leave the fruit to macerate in the wine in a cool place overnight.

● Serve the berries just as they are, with a bowl of fresh cream or crème fraîche and a plate of shortbread to add a crisp bite.

Ricotta with Strawberry Sauce

Ricotta is a lovely fresh cheese, slightly grainy in texture and not too strong. It makes a very light, unfussy pudding when served with a tangy fresh fruit sauce. You do not need to use the most perfect strawberries for the sauce, in fact the ones that get a little squashed in the bottom of the punnet are perfect since they will have lots of flavour but maybe not the best appearance. I find that this sauce goes with all sorts of things, it tastes wonderful poured over peaches or raspberries or simply served with ice cream.

450g (1lb) fresh ricotta cheese	**For the sauce**
10ml (2 teaspoons) runny honey	225g (8oz) strawberries
a very good pinch of freshly grated	juice of ½ lemon
nutmeg	60-90ml (4-6 tablespoons)
4 strawberries, to serve	elderflower cordial, honey or corn
	syrup

- Mix the ricotta cheese with the honey and nutmeg.

- Make the sauce: liquidize the strawberries together with the lemon juice and enough cordial to sweeten.

- Put a good spoonful of cheese in the middle of 4 serving plates and pour the sauce around. Decorate each serving with a strawberry.

Hot Apricot and Lemon Soufflé

This soufflé is the lightest thing and contains no fat. Look out for the best organic dried apricots you can buy. Hunza apricots are particularly good. You could use other dried fruit – peaches would work very well. As with all soufflés, these will not keep long once out of the oven, so perhaps try your soufflé skills on friends first before you delight guests at a more formal dinner party.

225g (8oz) dried apricots	30ml (2 tablespoons) unrefined caster
150ml (¼ pint) orange juice	sugar
grated rind and juice of ½ unwaxed	4 egg whites
lemon	pinch of cream of tartar
	5ml (1 teaspoon) cornflour

● Stew the dried apricots gently in the orange juice until they are soft, then drain them.

● In a food processor or liquidizer, blend the apricots with the lemon rind and juice and the sugar. Whisk the egg whites with the cream of tartar until stiff. Sift the cornflour and fold it into the egg whites. Fold the whites into the apricots and pour into a 1.5 litre (2½ pint) soufflé dish.

● Bake in a pre-heated moderate oven, 180°C, 350°F, Gas Mark 4, for 30-35 minutes or until puffed and golden brown.

● Serve immediately, with fromage frais, Greek yogurt, cream or ice cream.

Hot Plum Compote

You could use greengages, apricots or damsons for this recipe. I find the microwave is ideal for cooking fruit gently as I can use a minimum of water, the fruit will not break up and they do not collect a metallic taste. Serve the compote by itself, as part of a selection of puddings, or with a bowl of crème fraîche, fromage frais or whipped double cream flavoured with vanilla.

450g (1lb) ripe plums or other similar fruit	115-175g (4-6oz) unrefined caster sugar pinch of ground mixed spice

- Remove the stalks from the fruit and, if you prefer, take out the stones. In the case of apricots, these are worth breaking and the kernels kept to scatter over the fruit later.

- Arrange the fruit in a glass microwave dish and add just enough water to fill one-quarter of the dish. Cover with a lid and microwave or bake in a pre-heated moderate oven, 180°C, 350°F, Gas Mark 4, until tender.

- Add enough sugar to sweeten the compote and stir in the mixed spice at the last moment.

SUPPLIERS OF ORGANIC FOODS

There are four main routes to finding a supply of organic ingredients:

1 Check your local supermarket. Make sure that they know you want to buy organic ingredients and hopefully they will expand their range.

2 Ring around the organic, health food, farm shop or specialist food shops in your area to find out who supplies what.

3 Join a local 'box scheme' where you can collect a regular supply of the freshest seasonal vegetables, fruit and sometimes other ingredients on a weekly basis.

4 Contact an organic supplier who offers a national postal or delivery service.

For excellent information on the above, contact The Soil Association for their booklet, *Where to Buy Organic Food*, including £5 to cover packing and postage.

The Soil Association
Bristol House
40 Victoria
Bristol BS1 6BY
Tel 0117 929 0661 Fax 0117 925 2504
e-mail: soilassoc@gn.apc.org

Supermarkets

UK supermarkets have come a long way in relation to selling organic foods over the last two or three years. Today, they recognize that there is a strong consumer demand for organic foods. The problem is that supply is currently so limited that most of them are finding it very difficult to offer their customers either an adequate range of organic foods or continuity of supply throughout the year. In response, some are setting up producer clubs trying to increase production and to encourage more producers to convert to organic methods.

This is all good news but there are still some fundamental problems in the way supermarkets operate which should be of concern to people buying organic foods. Most are still not seriously committed to local purchasing as many would rather centralize their production and distribution as much as possible. This can operate against the interests of the small producer and the range and variety of fruit and vegetables and a growing number of organic dairy products. Marks & Spencer has just reintroduced organic foods; Safeway, who originally pioneered their introduction, still stocks them; and ASDA, Somerfield and CWS are increasingly committed too. If you look carefully, you will also be able to find cereals, beverages, baby foods, preserves and jams, flour and other cereal products, including bread, in an increasing number of supermarkets.

Shopping recommendations

- Look for fruit and vegetable products – most UK supermarkets now carry a reasonable range.

- Some – Sainsbury, Waitrose and Marks & Spencer – now have organic meat in their 'flagship' stores.

- Look out for the Soil Association symbol as your best means of identifying organic products. Many supermarkets carry the symbol on their shelf labels.

- If you cannot find what you are looking for, ask the store manager or customer care desk. They will register your request which will strengthen their commitment to organic buying!

Registered symbol schemes

As well as The Soil Association, there are a number of other registered schemes who will be able to provide information:

Organic Farmers and Growers Ltd (OF&G)
Biodynamic Agricultural Association (BDAA)
Scottish Organic Producers Association (SOPA)
Irish Organic Farmers & Growers Association (IOFGA)
UK Register of Organic Food Standards (UKROFS)

REGIONAL SUPPLIERS

NORTHERN IRELAND

Ballylagan Organic Farm – farm gate
12 Ballylagan Rd, Straid, Ballyclare, BT39 9NF (019603 22867)
Beef, lamb, seasonal vegetables

Camp Hill Holywood Organic Bakery – coffee shop and shop
8 Shore Rd, Holywood, Nr Belfast, BT18 0DB (01232 423203)
Vegetables, dairy, bread, coffee, grains

Eat Well – shop, home delivery and mail order
413 Lisburn Rd, Belfast, BT9 7AW (01232 664362)
Bread, fruit, vegetables, dairy, herbs, wholefoods

Life Tree – shop
37 Spencer Rd, Derry, BT47 1AA (01504 342845)
Bread, vegetables, meat, eggs, dairy, wholefoods, herbs

Nutmeg – shop
9 Lombard St, Belfast, BT1 1RB (01232 249984)
Limited range of fruit, vegetables, dairy, wholefoods

Organic Fine Foods – box scheme and home delivery
N Down (01247 456873)
Cheese, beef, lamb, bread, fruit, vegetables

Quintess Fence – shop, home delivery and mail order
327 Antrim Rd, Belfast, BT15 2HE (01232 742659)
Bread, meat , wholefoods

SCOTLAND

Border

Juniper Fine Foods – delivery (only to shops)
Unit 2 Broomhouses, Dryfe Rd, Lockerbie, DG11 2RF (01576 204410
Alcohol, bread, fruit, vegetables, eggs, dairy, wholefoods

Loch Arthur Creamery – farm shop and mail order
Beeswing, Dumfries, Dumfries & Galloway, DG2 8JQ (01387 760296)
Hard and soft cheeses, butter, meat

Sunrise Wholefoods – shop
49 King St, Castle Douglas, DG7 1AE (01556 504455
Alcohol, bread, fruit, vegetables, dairy, wholefoods

Central

Bellfield Organic Nursery– box scheme and home delivery
Strathmiglo, Fife, KY14 7RH (01337 860764)
Fruit, vegetables

Damhead Organic Farm – shop, home delivery and mail order
32a Damhead, Old Pentland Rd, Lothianburn, Edinburgh, EH10 7EA (0131 445 1490)
Meat, poultry, bread, fruit, vegetables, eggs, dairy wholefoods, herbs

Evergreen Wholefoods – shop
18 Nithsdale Rd, Pollockshields, Glasgow, G41 2AN (0141 422 1303)
Bread, ice cream, fruit, vegetables, eggs, wholefoods

Falkland, Cupar, Fife, KY15 7AD (01337 857749)
Beef, lamb, fruit, vegetables, dairy, wholefoods, herbs

Henderson's Farm – shop
92 Hanover St, Edinburgh, EH2 1DR (0131 225 6694)
Alcohol, bread, fruit, vegetables, eggs, dairy, wholefoods, herbs

Jamesfield Organic & Freerange Meats Ltd – shop, mail order and home delivery
Jamesfield Farm, Newburgh, Fife, KY14 6EW (01738 850498)
Vegetables, meat, bacon, pies, haggis, sausages

Nature's Gate – shop
83 Clerk St, Edinburgh, EH8 9JG (0131 668 2067)
Alcohol, bread, fruit, vegetables, eggs, dairy, wholefoods

Real Foods Ltd – shop and mail order
37 Broughton St, Edinburgh, EH1 3JU (0131 557 1911)
Alcohol, bread, fruit, vegetables, eggs, dairy, wholefoods

North

Cockles Shop
37 Lochnell St, Lochgilphead, PA31 8HJ (01546 606292)
Bread, dairy, herbs, wholefoods

Highland Wholefoods – regional delivery and cash & carry
Unit 6, 13 Harbour Rd, Inverness, IV1 1SY (01463 712393)
Alcohol, bread, fruit, vegetables, eggs, dairy, wholefoods, herbs

Jackson's Wholefoods – shop
Park Lane, Portree, Isle of Skye, IV51 9EP (01478 613326)
Small but expanding range of wholefoods

Millstone Wholefoods – shop and mail order
15 High St, Oban, PA34 4BG (01631 562704)
Bread, fruit, vegetables, eggs, dairy, wholefoods

Phoenix Community Stores – shop and mail order
The Park, Findhorn Bay, Moray, IV36 0T (01309 690110)
Meat, alcohol, bread, fruit, vegetables, eggs, dairy, wholefoods, herbs

Wheems Box Scheme – home delivery
Wheems, Eastside, South Ronaldsay, Orkney Islands, KW17 2TJ (01856 831537)
Vegetables

WALES

Mid-Wales

Graig Farm – farm shop and mail order
Dolau, Llandrindod Wells, LD1 5TL (01597 851655) also 07000 ORGANIC
Meat, poultry, pies, cakes, eggs, dairy, wholefoods, herbs

P A Knifton & A Degan – farm gate sales
Ty-Hen, Penbryn, Sarnau, Llandysul, SA44 6RD (01239 810347)
Milk and Gouda-style mature cheese

Primrose Farm – farm shop, box scheme and home delivery
Felindre, Brecon, LD3 0ST (01497 847636)
Fruit, vegetables

Rachel's Dairy – farm shop (limited hours, please phone)
Brynllys, Borth, SY24 5L (01970 871489)
Yogurt, cheese, cream, beefburger and beef mince

The Warren – local delivery
The Warren, New Radnor, Prestiegne, LD8 2TN (01544 350407)
Meat

Tree House – farm shop
Pier St, Aberystwyth (01970 820285)
Fruit, vegetables, meat, dairy

Welsh Organic Foods Ltd – mail order
20-21 Llanbedr Estate, Lampeter, SA48 8LT (01570 422772)
Soft cheeses, Pencarreg original and blue

North

Country Kitchen – shop,
10 Sea View Rd, Colwyn Bay, LL29 8DG (01492 533329)
Bread, fruit, vegetables, dairy, wholefoods

Delivery Discount Organics – market stall and home delivery
Flintshire (01352 740075)
Fruit, vegetables, meat

Dimension – shop
15 Holyhead Rd, Bangor, LL57 2EG (01248 370076)
Bread, fruit, vegetables, dairy, wholefoods, herbs

Rhosfawr Nurseries – farm shop
Rhosfawr, Pwllheli, LL53 6YA (01766 810545)
Vegetables

Ty Newydd Farm shop – home delivery
The Green, Denbigh (01745 812882)
Fruit, vegetables, dairy, wholefoods

South

Bwydydd Cyflawn Trefdraeth – shop
East Street, Newport, SA42 0SY (01239 820773)
Wine, fruit, vegetables, cheese, dairy, wholefoods

Caerfai Farm – farm shop (please phone)
St David's, Pembrokeshire, SA62 6QT (01437 720548)
Milk, cream, yogurt, cheese
Fruit and vegetables in summer

Irma Fingal-Rock – shop and home delivery
64 Monnow St, Monmouth, NP5 3EN (01600 712372)
Alcohol, bread, fruit, vegetables, eggs, dairy

Llwyn Ifan Ddu Farm – farm gate
Garnswllt Rd, Pontardulais, Swansea, SA4 1QJ (01269 592090)
Lamb, beef

Medhope Organic Growers – farm shop and box scheme
Tintern, Chepstow, NP6 7NX (01291 689797)
Fruit, vegetables, wholefoods, herbs

Pencoed Organic Growers – farm gate and box scheme
Felindre Nurseries, Pencoed, Bridgend, CF35 5HU (01656 861956)
Seasonal vegetables, salads, herbs

Pencrugiau Farm – shop (please phone)
Felindre, Crymych, Pembrokeshire, SA41 3XH (01239 881265)
Fruit, vegetables and salads in season

Pumpkin Shed – box scheme and home delivery
Cartref, Rhodiad y Brenin, St David's, Pembrokeshire, SA62 6PJ (01437 721949)
Cheese, fruit, vegetables

Rogerswell Farm Gate – box scheme and home delivery
Whitland, Pembrokeshire, SA34 0QY (01994 240237)
Fruit, vegetables, meat, dairy

Spice of Life – shop and box scheme
1 Inverness Place, Roath, Cardiff, CF2 4RU (01222 487146)
Dairy, wholefoods, herbs

Treiorwg Farm – shop
Treiorwg, Trap, Llandielo, SA19 6RF (01558 823037)
Meat

Upper Pant Farm – farm shop and delivery
Llandewi Rhydderch, Abergavenny, NP7 9TL (01873 858091)
Meat

Wye Valley Herbs – farm shop
The Nurtons, Tintern, Chepstow, NP6 7NX (01291 689253)
Pot-grown herbs

ENGLAND

LONDON

Bumblebee Shop
30, 32, 33 Brecknock Rd, London N7 0DD (0171 607 1936)
A full range of organic produce and products

Bushwacker Wholefoods – shop
132 King St, Hammersmith, London W6 0QU (0181 748 2061)
Bread, fruit, vegetables, eggs, dairy, wholefoods

C Lidgate Butcher – shop and deliveries
110 Holland Park Ave, London W11 4UA (0171 727 8243)
Beef, lamb

Food for Thought – shop
38 Market Place, Kingston upon Thames, KT1 1JQ (0181 546 7806)
Bread, fruit, vegetables, eggs, dairy, wholefoods

Haelan Centre – shop and mail order
41 The Broadway, Crouch End, London N8 8DT (0181 340 4258)
Bread, fruit, vegetables, eggs, dairy, wholefoodss, herbs

Just Organic – box scheme and home delivery
26 St Mary's Grove, London N1 2NT (0171 704 2566)
Fruit, vegetables

Planet Organic – shop
42 Westbourne Grove, London W2 5SH (0171 221 7171)
Supermarket selling vast range of organic food

Spitalfields Organic Market – market stall
65 Brushfield St, London E16AA (01279 444663)
Fruit, vegetables, poultry, dairy, wholefoods, bread, herbs, wine
Farmers and growers sell direct to public

The Fresh Food Company – mail order, home delivery and box scheme
326 Portobello Rd, London W10 5RU (0181 969 0351)
Wide selection of organic storecupboard ingredients, with meat, bread, dairy and vegetable box schemes

The Realfood Store – shop and home delivery
14 Clifton Rd, Little Venice, London W9 1SS (0171 266 1162)
Bread, fruit, vegetables, meat, eggs, dairy, wholefood, herbs

Whole Earth Foods Ltd – shop
269 Portobello Rd, London W11 1LR (0171 229 7545)
Large range of organic foods

Wholefood Ltd – shop
24 Paddington St, London WIM 4DR (0171 935 3924)
Wholefood, vegetables, bread, dairy

Wholefood Ltd – shop
31 Paddington St, London WIM 4DR (0171 486 1390)
Full range of organic produce and meat

Wild Oats Wholefoods – shop
210 Westbourne Grove, London W11 2RH (0171 243 0988)
A full range of organic ingredients

ENGLAND A - Z

Berkshire
Doves Farm Foods Ltd – farm gate and mail order
Salisbury Rd, Hungerford, Berkshire, RG17 0RF (01488 684880)
Flour, biscuits, cereals, baked goods

Ellis Organics – home delivery
Little Bottom Farm, Colliers Lane, Rotherfield Peppard, Nr Henley (01491 628889)
Poultry, meat, bread, fruit, vegetables, eggs, dairy

Garlands Farm – farm shop, home delivery and pick-your-own
Gardeners Lane, Upper Basildon, RG8 8NP (01491 671556)
Meat, poultry, alcohol, fruit, vegetables, eggs, dairy, special dietary foods

Birmingham
Organic Roots – farm shop and home delivery
Crabtree Farm, Dark Lane, Kings Norton, B38 OBS (01564 822294)
Bread, fruit, vegetables, meat, eggs, dairy, wholefoods

Bristol
The Better Food Company – home delivery
Leviathan, 1 Hobbs Lane, Barrow Gurney, Bristol, BS19 3SU (01275 474545)
Alcohol, fruit, vegetables, meat, wholefoods, herbs

Out of This World – shop
Clifton Down Shopping Centre, Whiteladies Rd, Clifton, BS8 2NN (0117 946 6909)
Meat, poultry, bread, fruit, vegetables, alcohol, wholefoods

Buckinghamshire
Brillbury Hall Farm Food
Brill, Bucks (01844 238407)

Claydon Organic Garden Farm – shop
Claydon House, Middle Claydon Buckingham, MK18 2EX (01296 738061)
Fruit, vegetables, herbs

The Organic Trail – box scheme and home delivery
25 York Rd, Stoney Stratford, Milton Keynes, MK11 1BJ (01908 568952)
Fruit, vegetables

Cambridgeshire
Arjuna Wholefoods – shop
12 Mill Rd, Cambridge, CD1 2AD (011223 364845)
Wine, bread, fruit, vegetables, eggs, dairy, wholefoods

Naturally Yours – box scheme and home delivery
The Horse and Gate Farm, Witcham Toll, Ely, CB6 1AB (01353 778723)
Vegetable boxes, meat, cheese, fruit, wholefoods

Wisbech Wholefoods – shop
8 North St, Old Market, Wisbech, PE13 1NP (01945 464468)
Fruit, vegetables, dairy, wholefoods, herbs, dried goods

Cheshire
Oakcroft Organic Gardens – market stall and box scheme
Cross O'The Hill, Malpas, SY14 8DH (01948 860213)
Bread to order, fruit, vegetables, eggs, dairy

Cornwall
Carleys – shop
34-36 Saint Austell St, Truro, Cornwall, TR1 1SE (01872 277686)
Alcohol, bread, fruit, vegetables, dairy, wholefoods, herbs

Stoneybridge Farm – shop
Stoneybridge Organic Nursery, Tywardreath, Par, PL24 2TY (01726 813858)
Meat, poultry, cheese, wine, fruit, vegetables, dairy, herbs

The Barn Farm Gate
The Barn, Leswidden, St Just, Penzance, TR19 7RU (01736 787953)
Vegetables, cheese, dairy, meat

Cumbria
Brambles Wholefoods – shop and home delivery
7 Bridge St, Appleby, CA16 6QH (01768 353588)
Bread, vegetables, dairy, wholefoods, herbs

EH Booth & Co Ltd – shop
The Old Station, Victoria St, Windermere (01539 446114)
Seasonal fruit and vegetables, dairy, bread, flour

Kan Foods – shop and box scheme
9 New Shambles, Kendal, LA9 4TS (01539
721190)
Fruit, vegetables, dairy, wholefoods, herbs

The Village Bakery Shop – box scheme and mail
order
Melmerby, Penrith, Cumbria, CA10 1HE (01768
881515)
Bread, pastries, pies, puddings, baking supplies
Fruit and vegetable boxes

Derbyshire
Lodge Farm – home delivery
Lodge Lane, Kirk Langley, DE6 4NX (01332
824815)
Beef, lamb

Market Wholefoods – shop and home delivery
The Shambles, 1a Mellor Rd, New Mills, High
Peak, Nr Stockport, SK22 4DW (01663 747550)
Alcohol, bread, fruit, vegetables, meat, eggs, dairy,
wholefoods

Organic Health – shop and mail order
23 Market St, Heanor, Derbyshire DE75 7NR
(01773 717718)
Alcohol, bread, fruit, vegetables, meat, eggs, dairy,
wholefoods, herbs

Devon
Higher Hacknell Farm – farm shop, box scheme
and mail order
Burrington, Umberleigh, EX37 9LX (01769 560292)
Potatoes, beef, lamb
Meat box scheme

Highfield Farm – shop, box scheme and home
delivery
Clyst Rd, Topsham, EX3 0BY (01392 876388)
Wine, fruit, vegetables, meat, dairy, wholefoods

Marshford Organic Nursery – farm shop and
market stall
Churchill Way, Northam, Nr Bideford, EX39 1NS
(01237 477160)
Bread, fruit, vegetables, meat, eggs, dairy,
wholefoods, herbs

Rocombe Farm Ice Cream – shop and mail order
123 Union St, Castle Circus, Torquay, Devon, TQ1
3DW (01803 293996)
Mail order (1626 872291)
Farm-fresh ice cream

West Country Organic Foods Ltd – mail order
Natson Farm, Tedburn St Mary, Exeter, EX6 6ET
(01647 24724)
Meat, poultry, wholefoods, grocery

Dorset
Down to Earth Shop – box scheme
18 Princes St, Dorchester, DT1 1TW (01305
268325)
Alcohol, bread, fruit, vegetables, dairy, wholefoods,
herbs

Gold Hill Organic Farm – farm shop, box scheme
and market stall
Child Okeford, Blandford, DT11 8HB (01258
860293)
Salads, fruit, winter vegetables, beef, dairy

Longmeadow Organic Vegetables – farm gate and
box scheme
Godmanstone, Dorchester, DT2 7AE (01300
341779)
Apples, vegetables

Essex
Happy Caterpillar – shop and home delivery
92 Leigh Rd, Leigh-on-Sea (01702 712982)
Fruit, vegetables, wholefoods

Mill Farm – farm gate (June-Nov)
Mill Lane, Purleigh, Chelmsford, CM3 6PU (01621
828280)
Vegetables

Pilgrims Natural Shop
41-43 High St, Halstead, CO9 2AA (01787
478513)
Bread, fruit, vegetables, eggs, dairy, wholefoods

Traders Fair – box scheme
10 High St, Old Harlow, CM17 0DW (01279
450908)
Fruit, vegetables

Gloucestershire
Hobbs House Bakery
39 High St, Chipping Sodbury, BS17 6BA (01454
321629)
Bread, pastries

Living Earth Produce – shop
Ruskin Mill, Old Bristol Rd, Nailsworth, GL6 0LA
(01453 834927)
Goat's milk and dairy, meat, bread, fruit,
vegetables, eggs, wholefoods

Slipstream Organics – box scheme, home delivery
and shop
34a Landon Rd, Cheltenham, GL53 7N (01242
227273)
Fruit, vegetables, herbs

Tetbury Traditional Meats – butcher
31 Church St, Tetbury, GL8 8JG (01666 502892)
Meat, from Highgrove when available

Hampshire
Harroway Organic Garden – farm gate
Kingsclere Rd, Whitchurch, RG28 7QB (01256
895346)
Fruit, vegetables, eggs, dairy, herbs

Park Farm – shop and farm shop
Park Farm, Heckfield, Hook, RG27 0LD (01189
326650)
Meat, poultry

Sunnyfields Organic Farm – shop and home
delivery
Jacob's Gutter Lane, Marchwood, Southampton,
SO40 9FX (01703 871408)
Fruit, bread, vegetables, meat, dairy, wholefoods,
alcohol

Hereford & Worcester
Dunkertons Cider Farm – shop, mail order and restaurant
Pembridge, Nr Leominster, HR6 9ED (01544 388653)
Cider, perry

Green Acres Organic Growers – farm shop
Dinmore, Hereford, HR4 8ED (01568 797045)
Seasonal vegetables, meat, herbs, eggs, jams

Greenlink Organic Foods – shop, box scheme and home delivery
9 Graham Rd, Malvern, WR14 2HR (01648 576266)
Poultry, cheese, juice, fruit, vegetables, meat, wholefoods

Prospect Organic Growers – farm shop
Prospect Cottage, Bartestree, Hereford, HR1 4BY (01432 851164)
Poultry, meat, bread, fruit, vegetables, eggs, dairy, wholefoods

Hertfordshire
Cook's Delight – shop, mail order and home delivery
360-4 High St, Berkhamsted, Hertfordshire, HP41 1HU (01442 863584)
Vegetables, macrobiotic foods, alcohol, bread, eggs, dairy, wholefoods, herbs

Eastwoods of Berkhamsted – shop and mail order
15 Gravel Path, Berkhamsted, HP4 2EF (01442 865012)
Butcher, also fruit, herbs, juice, biscuits

Full of Beans – shop
2 Church St, Sawbridgeworth, Hertfordshire (01279 726002)
Bread, fruit, vegetables, dairy, wholefoods

Kent
Canterbury Wholefoods – shop and home delivery
10 The Borough, Canterbury, CT1 2DR (01227 464623)
Alcohol, bread, fruit, vegetables, eggs, dairy, wholefoods, herbs

Luddesdown Organic Farms Ltd – farm gate, box scheme and home delivery
Court Lodge, Luddesdown, Nr Cobham, DA13 0XE (01474 813376)
Vegetables, beef

Yalding Organic Gardens (HDRA) – shop and box scheme
Benover Rd, Yalding, Nr Maidstone, ME18 6EX (01622 814650)
Wholefoods, seasonal fruit and vegetables

Lancashire
Growing with Nature – box scheme and home delivery
Bradshaw Lane Nursery, Pilling, Preston, PR3 6AX (01253 790046)
Fruit, vegetables

Red Rose Organics – box scheme and home delivery
14 Bluebell Ave, Helmshore, Rossendale, BB4 6NF (01706 226189)
Bread, vegetables, wholefoods

Leicestershire
Chevelswarde Organic Growers – farm shop and box scheme
Chevel House, The Belt, South Kilworth, Lutterworth, LE17 6DX (01858 575309)
Local wine, flour, vegetables, fruit, eggs

Dennis Brewin Quality Food – shop
26/27 High St, Loughborough, LE11 2P (01509 215260)

Meat Growing Concern – farm shop and mail order
Home Farm, Woodhouse, Lane, Nanpanton, Loughborough, LE11 3YG (01509 239228)
Rare breeds meat. Smokehouse and bakery, game, poultry, cheese, sausages, eggs, fruit, vegetables

Lincolnshire
Barrow and Goxhill Organic Growers – box scheme and farm gate
3 Thorngarth Lane, Barrow on Humber, DN19 7AW (01469 530721)
Vegetables, fruit, herbs

Holbeach Wholefood – shop
32 High St, Holbeach, Nr Spalding, P12 7DY (01406 422149)
Bread, fruit, vegetables, wholefoods

Spice of Life – shop and box scheme
4 Burghley Centre, Bourne, PE10 9EG (01778 394735)
Bread, fruit, vegetables, wholefoods

Manchester
Limited Resources – box scheme and home delivery
53 Old Birley St, Hulme, M15 5RF (0161 226 4777)
Alcohol, fruit, vegetables, eggs, dairy, wholefoods

On the Eight Day Co-operative Ltd – shop and café
107-111 Oxford Rd, M1 7DU (0161 273 4878)
Alcohol, bread, vegetables, dairy, wholefoods

Unicorn Grocery Ltd – shop
89 Albany Rd, Chorlton, Manchester, M21 0BN (0161 861 0010)
Alcohol, bread, fruit, vegetables, wholefoods, herbs

Norfolk
Camphill Communities East Anglia – box scheme
Thornage Hall, Holt, NR25 7QH (01263 861481)
Vegetable boxes, meat

Domini Quality Foods – farm gate (please phone)
H F Capon & Son, Village Farm, Market Weston, Diss, IP22 2N (01359 221333)
Dairy, meat, poultry, grains, flour, eggs

Traditional Norfolk Poultry – farm gate, mail order and home delivery
33 Thetford Rd, Watton, Thetford, Norfolk, IP425 6BX (01953 885404)
Bronze turkeys, chickens

Northamptonshire
Goodness Foods – shop
78-80 High St, Braunston, Daventry, NN11 7HS
(01788 890305)
Wholefoods , bread

Northumberland
The Green Shop – mail order and box scheme
54 Bridge St, Berwick upon Tweed,
Northumberland, TD15 1AQ (01289 330897)
Fruit and vegetable box scheme, eggs, dairy,
wholefoods, herbs

North East Organic Growers – box scheme and
farm gate
Earth Balance, West Sleekburn Farm, Bormarsund,
Bedlington, NE22 7AD (01665 575785)
Vegetables, herbs

Nottinghamshire
Awsworth Nurseries Shop
Awsworth Lane, Cossall, Nottinghamshire, NG16
2R (01159 442545)
Bread, fruit, vegetables, meat, eggs, dairy,
wholefoods, herbs, salads

Barn Farm – shop and B & B
Barn Farm Cottage, Kneeton Rd, East Bridgeford,
NG13 8PJ (01949 20196)
Meat, poultry, bread, fruit, vegetables, eggs, dairy,
wholefoods, herbs

Out of this World – shop
Unit Four, Villa St, Beeston, Nottingham, NG9 2NY
(01159 431311)
Alcohol, bread, fruit, vegetables, eggs, dairy,
wholefoods, meat, poultry

Oxfordshire
Meat Matters – home delivery and mail order
2 Blandy's Farm Cottages, Letcombe Regis,
Wantage, OC12 9LI (01235 762461)
Range of meats, roasting joints, poultry, sausages,
bacon, gammon, ham, eggs

Frugal Food – shop
17 West Saint Helen St, Abingdon, OX14 5BI
(01235 522239)
Vegetables, alcohol, bread, dairy, wholefoods

The Old Dairy – farm shop
Path Hill Farm, Whitchurch on Thames, RG8 7RE
(01734 842392)
Alcohol, bread, fruit, vegetables, eggs, dairy,
wholefoods, herbs, meat, poultry

Shropshire
Broad Bean Shop – mail order and box scheme
60 Broad St, Ludlow, Shropshire, SY8 1NH (01584
874239)
Fruit and vegetable boxes, alcohol, bread, meat,
eggs, dairy, wholefoods

Pimhill Farm – farm shop
Lea Hall, Hamer Hill, Shrewsbury, SY4 3DY (01939
290342)
Meat, flour, cereals, honey, bread, baking, cheese,
fruit, vegetables, eggs

Shropshire Hills Organic Produce – box scheme
and home delivery
Bentley House, Clungunford, Nr Craven Arms, SY7
0PN (01588 660255)
Honey, cheese, fruit, vegetables, eggs

Somerset
Ceres Natural Foods – shop and box scheme
42 Prices St, Yeovil, BA20 1ED (01935 428791)
Fruit, vegetables, alcohol, bread, dairy, wholefoods,
herbs

Hambleden Herbs – mail order
Court Farm, Milverton, Somerset, TA41 NF (01823
401205)
Herbs, spices

Merrick Organic Farm – box scheme
Langport, Somerset (01458 252901)
Meat, vegetables

Swaddles Green Farm – farm gate (please phone)
and UK home delivery
Hare Lane, Buckland St Mary, Chard, Somerset ,
TA20 3JR (01460 234387)
Meat, poultry, beer, wine, cheese, butter, prepared
meals

The Wholefood Store – shop
29 High St, Glastonbury, BA6 9SDR (01458
831004)
Alcohol, bread, fruit, vegetables, eggs, dairy,
wholefoods

Staffordshire
Staffordshire Organic Cheeses – farm shop
Newhouse Farm, Acton, Newcastle under Lyme,
ST5 4EE (01782 680366)
Cheese, meat, beer, wines

The Good Food Shop – shop, box scheme and
home delivery
475-477 Hartshill Rd, Hartshill, Stoke on Trent ,
ST4 6AA (01782 710234)
Meat, poultry, alcohol, bread, fruit, vegetables,
eggs, dairy, wholefoods

Suffolk
Barleycorn Wholefoods – home delivery and mail
order
Crake Hall, High Common, Clarkes Lane,
Barsham, Beccles, Suffolk, NR34 8HW
(01502 715637)
Bread, fruit, vegetables, eggs, dairy, wholefoods,
herbs, meat to order

Longwood Farm – farm shop, market stall, mail
order and deliveries
Tuddenham St Mary, Bury St Edmunds, Suffolk,
IP28 6TB (01638 717120)
Beef, lamb, pork, poultry, bacon, fruit, vegetables,
dairy, wholefoods, cheese, Christmas specialities

Pure Organic Foods – home delivery and mail
order
PO Box 7, Leiston, Suffolk, IP16 4XQ (01 728
830575)
Poultry, cheese, bacon, sausages, salami, pâté,
ham, eggs, pies

Surrey
Epsom Downs Friends of Organic Farmers – box
scheme
73 Shawley Way, Epsom Downs, KT18 5PD
(01737 359620)
Fruit, vegetables

Octavia's Organic Pantry – shop
7 Prices Lane, Woodhatch, Reigate, RH2 HBB
(01737 244155)
Meat, poultry, bread, fruit, vegetables, eggs, dairy,
wholefoods

Sussex
Boathouse – farm shop
Boathouse Organic Farm, Isfield, Uckfield, TN22
5TY (01825 750302)
Meat, potatoes, flour, fruit, dairy, wholefoods,
herbs

Finbarr's Wholefoods – shop, home delivery and
box scheme
57 George St, Hastings, TN34 3EE (01424
443025)
Alcohol, bread, fruit, vegetables, eggs, dairy,
wholefoods

Seasons Forest Row Ltd – shop
10 Hartfield Rd, Forest Row, RH18 5DN (01342
824673)
Organic and biodynamic produce
Bread, fruit, vegetables, meat, eggs, dairy,
wholefoods

Warwickshire
Ryton Garden Visitor Centre – restaurant, shop and
box scheme
Henry Doubleday Research Association, Ryton
Organic Gardens, Coventry, CV8 3LG (01203
308201)
Meat, fish, poultry, alcohol, bread, fruit, vegetables,
eggs, dairy, wholefoods, herbs

Wiltshire
Eastbrook Farm – farm shop, home delivery and
mail order
Bishopstone, Swindon, Wiltshire, SN69PW (01793
790460)
Meat, poultry, eggs, sausages, pies, cured meats

Malmesbury Whole Foods – shop and home
delivery
29 Abbey Row, Malmesbury, SN16 0AG (01666
823030)
Fruit, vegetables, eggs, dairy, wholefoods, bread,
flour

Pertwood Organics Co-op – box scheme
Lower Pertwood Farm, Hinden, Salisbury, SP3
6PA (01747 820763)
Fruit, vegetables

Yorkshire
Bradford Wholefoods – shop and box scheme
78 Morley St, Bradford, BD7 1AQ (01274 307539)
Local fruit and vegetables, bread, eggs, dairy,
wholefoods

Goosemoorganics – box scheme
Warfield Lane, Cowthorpe, Wetherby, Leeds, LS22
5EU (01423 358887)
Bread, salad, fruit, vegetables, eggs, dairy,
wholefoods

Simply Organic – farm shop
Sandylands, Market Weighton Rd, Barlby, Selby,
YO8 7LB (01757 708540)
Poultry, meat, bread, fruit, vegetables, eggs, dairy,
wholefoods

The Green House – shop and home delivery
5 Station Parade, Harrogate, HG1 1UF (01423
502580)
Alcohol, bread, fruit, vegetables, eggs, dairy

Vin Ceremos Wines and Spirits Ltd + HDRA
Organic Wine Club – shop
261 Upper Town St, Leeds, LS13 3JT (0113 257
7545)
Wine, beer, cider, fruit juice, spirits, olive oil,
cordials

INDEX

INDEX

avgolemono, 10
chargrilled chicken fajitas, 123-4
chargrilled chicken salad, 53
chicken satay with peanut and
coconut sauce, 29
chicken with lemon, honey and
garlic, 119
chicken with spinach and tamari,
132
cinnamon chicken with almonds,
121
Thai green chicken curry, 127
chickpeas:
alfalfa and chickpea salad with
ginger and sesame dressing,
44
felafel, 66
houmous, 20
chill-out chocolate cake, 166
chillies:
chicken satay with peanut and
coconut sauce, 29
crispy Thai prawns, 35
fiery cod and mussel casserole,
93
loin of pork with chillies, 112
red curry paste, 85
chocolate:
chill-out chocolate cake, 166
chocolate pots, 168
double chocolate chip cookies,
149
chowder, salmon with prawns, 6
cinnamon chicken with almonds,
121
clafoutis, cherry, 164
classic Welsh country soup, 5
coconut milk:
chicken satay with peanut and
coconut sauce, 29
Thai green chicken curry, 127
cod:
fiery cod and mussel casserole,
93
fish and chips, 83
seafood in saffron sauce with
garlic potatoes, 92
Thai fish in red curry, 85

cookies, double chocolate chip,
149
coriander:
carrot and coriander soup, 16
pork with red wine and coriander,
114
seared tuna with coriander and
rice noodles, 97
venison with coriander seeds and
leek and potato rösti, 122
courgette flowers, stuffed, 77
courgettes:
couscous with Mediterranean
vegetables, 65
marinated grilled vegetables, 51
couscous:
couscous with Mediterranean
vegetables, 65
tagine of lamb with couscous,
111
crab:
dressed crab with lemon
mayonnaise, 90
cracked wheat:
cracked wheat and herb salad,
45
Cypriot raisin pilaff, 67
cream:
chill-out chocolate cake, 166
chocolate pots, 168
gooseberry cream with
elderflower, 159
crème fraîche:
carrot cake with lemon crème
fraîche, 141
crispy Thai prawns, 35
crostini, 33
goat's cheese, 8
croûtons, 53
cucumber:
Greek village salad, 43
iced ripe tomato and garlic soup,
4
zatziki, 23
currants:
Welsh cakes, 147
curries:
red curry paste, 85

COOK'S NOTES

Join the Soil Association

Yes I want to join and help promote organic food production and preserve the health of the countryside.

Name ....

Address ....

....

....

Postcode .... Phone ....

Membership categories (please tick as appropriate)

Individual   ☐   £18.00   Life   ☐   £500.00

Joint   ☐   £25.00   Senior Citizen   ☐   £10.00

Unwaged   ☐   £10.00

I include a donation of: £20 ☐   £25 ☐   £50 ☐   Other ☐

I enclose my cheque made payable to the Soil Association for

£ .... Please debit my Visa/Access Card No.

☐☐☐☐   ☐☐☐☐   ☐☐☐☐   ☐☐☐☐

Expiry date   ☐☐   ☐☐

Name on card .... Date ....

Return to: The Soil Association, Freepost (BS4456) Bristol BS1 5YZ

The Soil Association is a registered Charity No. 206862